Captured at Kut:
Prisoner of the Turks

Captured at Kut:

Prisoner of the Turks

The Great War Diaries of
Colonel W C Spackman

edited by
Tony Spackman

Foreword by Field Marshal Sir John Chapple,
GCB, CBE, DL

Pen & Sword
MILITARY

First published in Great Britain in 2008 by
Pen & Sword Military
an imprint of
Pen & Sword Books Ltd
47 Church Street
Barnsley
South Yorkshire
S70 2AS

A CIP catalogue record for this book is available from the British Library.

Typeset in Palatino Linotype by
Lamorna Publishing Services

Pen & Sword Books Ltd. incorporates the imprints of Pen & Sword Aviation,
Pen & Sword Maritime, Pen & Sword Military, Remember When
Publications, Wharncliffe Local History, Pen & Sword Select, Pen & Sword
Military Classics and Leo Cooper.

Printed and bound in England by CPI UK.

For a complete list of Pen & Sword titles please contact
PEN & SWORD BOOKS LIMITED
47 Church Street, Barnsley, South Yorkshire, S70 2AS, England
E-mail: enquiries@pen-and-sword.co.uk
Website: www.pen-and-sword.co.uk

Contents

Introduction

I have written this book for myself. I have written it with gusto. Each chapter contains memories I like to recall and relive, even in the depressing, desperate or tragic ones as a prisoner of war in Turkish hands; but more especially the gay, colourful and adventurous times it has been my exceptional good fortune to encounter in India and elsewhere, a selection of which I have included.

If others enjoy reading my book, so much the better!

W.C.S.

Foreword

by

Field Marshal Sir John Chapple
GCB CBE DL

Colonel W.C. Spackman, in his introduction, states that he wrote this account 'with gusto'. It is easy to see why. It tells of 'colourful and adventurous times' and is told with both gusto and modesty.

The first part presents a view of military action in Mesopotamia as seen by a young Medical Officer of the Indian Army, serving with a Regiment who were both combat infantry and pioneers.

The story then covers the Siege of Kut and its surrender, followed by a year or so as a prisoner of war but one who was required to look after the sick and wounded prisoners who remained in Mesopotamia. During this period, when he was largely on his own, he was able to observe life around him in Mosul and Baghdad and elsewhere in what is now Iraq. For much of this time he was deemed to be 'on parole'.

He was finally moved to Anatolia for the last part of the war where he met again the surviving officers and men with whom he had served at Kut.

There have been many records, both official and personal, of the campaign in Mesopotamia; and more than a few accounts of the siege and surrender of Kut. However there are very few records of what was happening in Baghdad, Mosul and other parts of the Ottoman Empire behind the front line. Young Lieutenant Spackman gives us a flavour of what it was like and of the very varied communities who were still continuing to 'do business' despite the war going on around them.

It took the British nearly four years fighting up the Tigris and Euphrates to reach Mosul. It took little more than four days in the second Gulf War for the US Forces to reach there.

The Turks were a tough enemy. Records of this campaign naturally have much to say about them. In most official records, there is hardly a mention of the local inhabitants whom we fought over, around and through. W.C. Spackman tells us a great deal about the local people and their daily lives. He was able to draw local currency by issuing a cheque or equivalent. He mentions the Jewish, Armenian and Chaldean Christians in Basra; the caravans coming into Amara 'almost daily' from Luristan, Kurdistan and Central Asia; The Persians, Kurds, Bakhtiaris, Lurs, Sabeans and Greeks as well as the local Arabs. There is also mention of the settled and nomadic Arabs, many of whom were dangerous marauders waiting to sweep in after a battle to kill, loot and pillage. These observations have historical value.

The author also knows his history well. He knew the location of the Garden of Eden, of Jonah's Tomb, Ezra's Tomb, Sennacherib's Palace, Saladin's birthplace and the Ur of the Chaldees.

A unique feature is the year or so he spent outside a prison camp looking after the wounded in Baghdad and Mosul. Not only did this provide an opportunity to meet local people but it allowed him to observe and comment on the Turkish Commanders.

His rather casual reference to his own bout of malaria and his acceptance of the scourge of scurvy, dysentery and other complaints reflects how much has changed in the past hundred years. Overall health hazards have greatly reduced but some things have also been lost - for instance the knowledge that the Arabs and Indian soldiers had about the local herbs which could be used beneficially.

The regimental medical officers of the day moved forward

close behind the attacking troops. They were very much in the firing line. The close relationship of this young twenty-six year old Lieutenant with his soldiers of the 48th Pioneers is taken for granted, because this was the natural relationship between British officers and their soldiers in the Indian Army.

Bill Spackman lodged his diaries with the Imperial War Museum, but until now the complete story has not been available. It is a worthy addition to the historical records, and a fascinating read.

Glossary

Araba	4 wheel covered cart
Bellums	Large canoes
Bhisties	Water carriers
Caserne	Billet for soldiers in a town or barracks
Chaoush	Sergeant
Danaks	A tribal name
Drabis	Mule attendants
Guffa	Round small craft like a coracle
Hajji	A Moslem who has made a pilgrimage to Mecca
Havildar	Sepoy Sergeant
Kanchi	Keeper of a khan
Keleks	Rafts
Khan	Village accommodation hostel
Kulla	A conical cap around which a turban is tied
Locantas	Restaurant
Mahelas	Arab dhows
Mashoofs	Light coracles
Mess	Officers' Mess
Mezzah	Appetizer
Onbashi	Corporal
Posta	Military guard
Raki	A strong spirit distilled from grain flavoured with aniseed.
RAMC	Royal Army Medical Corps
RAP	Regimental Aid Post
Reamur	A medical instrument
RMO	Regimental Medical Officer
Safa	Turban
Sepoy	Indian native soldier in British service
Serai	A caravanserai or inn
Shamaal	Strong desert wind
Vali	Local Mayor
Yakdan	A woollen rug placed under a saddle

Preface

by
Colonel Anthony Spackman
Royal Artillery

This is, in the first part, an account of the experiences of my uncle, William Collis Spackman, known to me as Uncle Bill, Will to his family, as a young Regimental Medical Officer with the 48th Pioneers, Indian Army, in the campaign in Mesopotamia during 1914 to 1916. A campaign which, for the 6th (Indian) Division and attached troops, under Major General Townshend, ended in disaster and, for many, death, in the Siege of Kut. After a siege lasting 147 days, longer than the Siege of Ladysmith, the 12,000 troops who surrendered were forced to march over 1,000 miles to their prison camps in Turkish Anatolia, more than half of them dying on the route. Of the 2,500 British officers and other ranks captured at Kut, only 700 returned two and a half years later.

The second part details, with stark realism but with a keen sense of humour, the treatment meted out to the prisoners of the Turks, the experiences and near disasters my uncle personally suffered between the surrender and his reaching the prison camp and finally his account of life in the prison camp in which he was held for the last seven months of the war.

Not long out of medical school at St Bartholomew's Hospital, he went to India as a young subaltern in January 1914 and joined the Indian Medical Service. After a summer enjoying life in the Regimental Mess of the 103rd Mahrattas at Ahmednagar he found himself, aged 25, shipped on the 16 October 1914 as Regimental Medical Officer to the 48th Pioneers with 16 Brigade of the 6th (Poona) Indian Division to Basra on the Persian Gulf, now part of Iraq but then part of the Turkish (Ottoman) Empire. The Division was part of a force tasked with driving the Turks, Allies of Germany, back into the interior towards Baghdad and securing Basra and its hinterland for the Allies. He kept a diary up to the fall of Kut al Amara, which was preserved, and then kept records of all his subsequent adventures from which, over the last years of his life (he died in 1975, aged 86), he compiled this account of his experiences.

I have not altered the structure of the narrative, nor any of its essential details and have not attempted to give the reader opinions about the higher management, or mismanagement, of the campaign. I think it better to leave the reader with the impressions of a junior non-combatant officer who viewed the campaign from rifle company level and who records what the rank and file think about the battles and siege in which he was personally involved. I have attempted to clarify the narrative and rephrase it but I trust that I have not changed it to alter the way my uncle intended it to read. Sadly, I did not know of the diary during his lifetime so I was not able to discuss any of its detail with him. For those who wish to follow the campaign, I have added a postscript giving a brief summary of what happened in that part of the Middle East before and after the fall of Kut. (See Appendix 2.)

My father, Dr Charles Spackman, also served as a medical officer throughout the First World War and, as is mentioned in this narrative, was attached to the 1st Battalion, Manchester Regiment, which was part of the unsuccessful Relief Force which suffered horrific casualties in trying to relieve Kut. The third brother, Maurice, served on the Western Front for the last two years of the war as an officer in the Royal Field Artillery. Luckily, all three, a fourth brother and an elder sister all survived to ripe old ages, averaging 87 years of age!

When the First World War ended and he was repatriated, Uncle Bill married his pre-war beloved and returned with his wife, Audrey, to the North-West Frontier Province in India. He came back to the UK in 1929 and, after qualifying FRCS (Gynaecology) at Edinburgh, returned to India where he remained, finally becoming Director, Medical Services, Bihar Province, until leaving India in 1945, to be employed by the Allied Relief Commission in Italy.

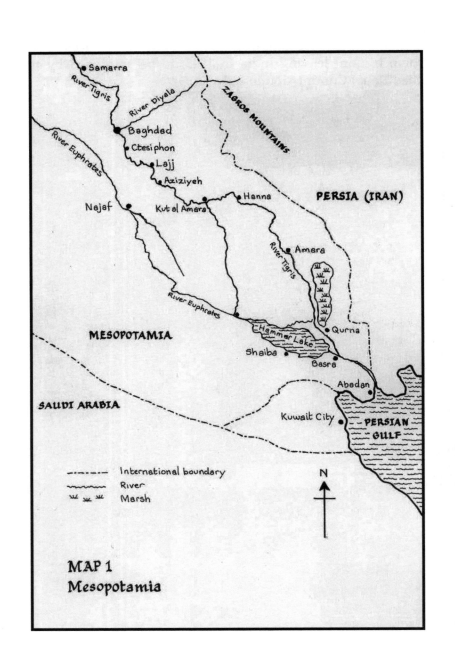

Samarra

River Tigris

River Diyala

ZAGROS MOUNTAINS

Baghdad
Ctesiphon
Lajj
Aziziyeh

River Euphrates

Najaf

Kut al Amara

Hanna

PERSIA (IRAN)

River Tigris

Amara

River Euphrates

MESOPOTAMIA

Hammar Lake

Qurna

Shaiba

Basra

SAUDI ARABIA

Abadan

Kuwait City

PERSIAN GULF

- · - · - · - International boundary
~~~~~~~~ River
ᵚᵚᵚ Marsh

N

MAP 1
Mesopotamia

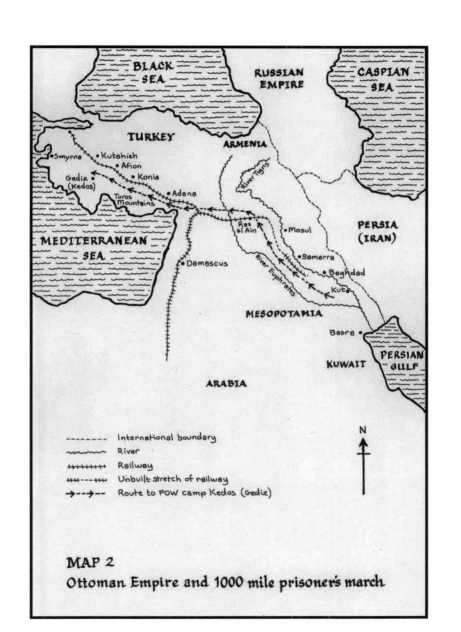

MAP 2
Ottoman Empire and 1000 mile prisoner's march

Chapter One

The Taking of Basra

My story does not concern itself, except briefly and in general terms, with the military strategy of the campaign in Mesopotamia, of which so much has already been written, but rather relates to one young and rather brash doctor in the frontline in that exciting and spectacularly disastrous phase which included the terrible Battle of Ctesiphon, the siege and fall of Kut al Amara, and my resulting strange adventures as a prisoner of war in the hands of the Turks.

After dodging the German cruiser/raider, the *Emden*, in our voyage across the Indian Ocean and then up the Persian Gulf, we landed from our transports a few miles up on the right bank of the Shatt al-Arab, that great river formed by the confluence of the Rivers Tigris and Euphrates, in the face of only slight resistance. Our immediate object was the protection of the Anglo-Persian oil refinery at Abadan.

My appreciation of the duties and responsibilities of a Regimental Medical Officer (RMO) on active service, and how to perform them as we advanced against the enemy on that early morning in November 1914, was extremely vague, not to say light-hearted, and an additional problem was that they were derived from Field Service Regulations framed for the South African War fifteen years earlier. None of us in the regiment had any experience of actual angry war, nor of what we were in for during the next four years.

My small medical unit, part of the splendid regiment of the British Indian Army, the 48th Pioneers, consisted of myself, fresh from hospital training at St Bartholomew's Hospital, London, inexperienced but very conscious of the Red Cross brassard over the left arm of my smart clean military tunic, an elderly henna-bearded Mohammedan medical assistant named Wali Ullah and a dozen Sikh stretcher bearers, ex-bandsmen. The stretchers and medical panniers were carried on pack mules in charge of 'drabis', Indian specialists in their limited duties but as yet liable to become flustered, like their charges, under the sudden impact and uproar of battle.

This small medical sub-unit advanced that day across the open desert, close behind our regiment which was deployed by companies as part of a force of mixed British and Indian troops of the 6th Indian Division, Indian Expeditionary Force, part of the well-trained Indian Army.

Suddenly and unexpectedly we came under a burst of artillery fire. Each shrapnel shell burst above us in a cloud of white smoke and a clatter of shot and fragments of shell fell all around. I found the shriek and violence of the shells catching one nakedly in the open, most alarming and my poor mules and drabis were scattered in some confusion, though little damage was done. We had none of the battle inoculation which formed so valuable a part of the training in the Second World War, when units were put into prepared trenches to be deliberately fired at by heavy batteries and nests of machine guns carefully ranged to fire short or over (though subject to occasional miscalculations) which taught soldiers that the terrific level of noise is by far the most unsettling feature of any encounter. We were still at the stage of ducking at the sound of the whine of a shell or the whistle of a bullet, not fully realizing that it was highly unlikely that any of these individual missiles could have one's name on it. In later battles one heard the deafening supersonic crack of a rifle fired at short range directly at one, breaking the sound barrier. This was really terrifying and twice I was caught accidentally in the open, exposed to the fire of our own 18-pounder field guns where the velocity was greater than sound and you had no time react to it. I was very fortunate only to be hit once in the campaign. Several RMOs I knew were killed or severely wounded; a sad waste of highly trained doctors.

But I must return to the battle below Basra. By the time I had ingloriously reassembled my unit in the dust and haze, we had lost contact with my 48th Pioneers. I caught a stray horse and, galloping forward to locate them among the advancing infantry, was able, in due course, to establish a small Regimental Aid Post (RAP) as laid down in Field Regulations! Here we collected our wounded and knocked up a rather feeble attempt at a shelter to try to provide protection from stray bullets. Some 100 casualties came walking, crawling or stretcher-borne to the RAP.

At one stage or another I had time to admire, and take heart from, the stirring sight of our horse-drawn field batteries galloping into action in Royal Tournament style, swinging their guns and limbers into line and, in what seemed mere seconds, finding and ranging onto the opposing Turkish guns which they soon silenced with ear-splitting explosions. It was even more thrilling in later battles to see S Battery, of the famous Royal Horse Artillery, operating in broken country with their lighter, more mobile guns, leaping and bounding in clouds of dust as the gun crews dashed forward, swung the guns round, unhitched the horses and took them sweating to the rear. How the gunners and drivers kept their seats I cannot imagine!

In my improvised dressing station on the battlefield I did what I could for each case, applying splints and dressings and giving injections or tablets of morphine to the worst wounded, then marking the dose on a label before they were taken back for treatment by the Field Ambulance following up the battle. I particularly remember one well-known senior Captain of the Dorset Regiment, who wore a monocle. He was found lying out in the sand severely wounded and in great pain. In his agony, as by habit, he screwed his monocle into his eye. I did what I could to make him comfortable but he rapidly grew weaker and paler until he sank lifeless. As he drew his last gasping breath his monocle fell from his eye upon the desert sand. My regiment alone lost thirteen sepoys killed and seventy wounded, with one officer suffering a fractured thigh.

We were soon in possession of the Turkish trenches, centred on an old fort on the edge of the line of date palms that marked the river bank. These palms had deprived us of direct support from the guns mounted on the naval vessels deployed in the river. When my little unit followed up into the position we had captured, I found many enemy wounded, some very severely, and was kept busy dealing with them. I snatched a sort of rough meal prepared by our Indian Mess cook, washed down by a nauseating concoction of rum and muddy Tigris water drunk out of an aluminium jug.

We were greeted with the distressing news that a sudden storm in mid-afternoon, almost unnoticed during the fighting, had sunk a lot of the dhows (mahelas) which were being used to transport our kit and Officers' Mess stores from the ships to the river bank. I lost the whole of my field kit and, like many others, had to make do for several days thereafter in what I stood up in or could scrounge or borrow. The men also lost most of their kits and cooking pots and a lot of ration stores, but there was no shortage of fire wood in the form of stalks and stumps of palm leaves. I spent that night dirty and cold, huddled in a shallow trench, unpleasantly like a grave, between two smelly sepoys, but being very tired, dozed off at intervals till dawn when we got more organized and were revived with tea. What would the British do in war and peace without a cup of tea?

Forward reconnaissance revealed that the Turks were abandoning Basra. Disorder was feared in this important town, the main port for the whole of Mesopotamia, famed in olden times as Balsora from whence Sinbad the Sailor set forth on his fabulous voyages.

The march on Basra started at 2000 hrs next night, 20 November 1914, in total darkness. The route was across desert ground without landmarks and intersected by a few creeks and marshy hollows. We relied on the local Arab guides who seemed none too reliable or unanimous. Our horses had been swum ashore from the transports. After about two miles my old syce collapsed so I put him up on my horse and marched nearly all night with the men, dozing off on my back on the damp ground at the frequent halts while the guides decided on the best route. Our Pioneers and the Sappers built small bridges or ramps for the guns and mule carts, a very tiresome proceeding for us as one never knew if the halt would be for five minutes or

4

for an hour. At dawn we halted while the Sappers put up a wireless mast to communicate with the ships which had, by now, reached Basra. I found the all night march most tiresome and monotonous, the whole thing becoming a blur of mirages once the morning sun rose higher and got hotter. We distinctly saw the masts of steamers magnified on the horizons but after going towards them for miles they flickered and disappeared. Any slight hollow in the desert ahead appeared to look like a pool of water with the leading troops wading in it. At one final halt about noon, in blazing heat, I fell asleep on the sand and my helmet fell off. I woke with a fierce headache which recurred in a milder form for years afterwards whenever I went hatless in the tropical sun.

After a march of about thirty miles, we camped in a grove of date palms by the Khora creek in Basra with a large crowd of Arabs looking on. The rougher types in the population were not pleased by our arrival as they had expected to profit by disorders in the town after the Turks had withdrawn. A number of such ruffians were to be seen next day suspended from a gallows in the main open space in the town. On the other hand, the large Jewish, Armenian and Chaldean Christian community gave us a most heartfelt and friendly welcome, not only grateful for the safety of their lives and properties but also for the prospect of much profit and renewed trade to come, amply fulfilled thereafter. There were plenty of black Ethiopians and Somalis available for heavy labour, capable of carrying immense loads on their backs. One heard talk in Arabic, Persian, French, Turkish, English and Italian, in about that order of frequency. Local supplies were plentiful and the usual camp market sprang up at once for purveyors of fresh produce of which our Mess cook took immediate advantage, though there was a wide variation as to prices and currencies. The Basra population was about 60,000.

My regiment was at first accommodated in a fine large building but as part of it turned out to be a mosque we moved elsewhere, including, for us officers, into the house of the former German manager of the great Wonkhaus Company. It had been pretty well denuded of contents except for a leaky bath and a very out-of-tune piano, with player attachment and two or three torn music rolls, but there was a cooking range for our cook. I recorded in my diary that I patched up the bath and had a thorough wash, up on the roof, the first for several days and much needed! I also made profitable trips to the main shops for stores for the Mess, for a toothbrush for myself and for many other items lost in the storm that took place downriver. The German Consulate proved to be a good prize especially as it contained a lot of very good German beer! Basra was the Eastern terminal of the great German dream, their 'Drang nach Osten' which included the projected Baghdad Railway connecting Constantinople (now Istanbul) with the Persian Gulf, the construction of which had scarcely started at that time. Their regional agent was the exceedingly able but wily Herr Wassmuss who gave us great trouble on account of his political activities on behalf of the Persians. The drive to the East was subsequently taken over as an objective by the Russians. The river was very tidal, all the many creeks filling and emptying twice daily and all the little river craft, bellums (large canoes) and small dhows being kept very busy. However, not surprisingly, the water supply being drawn only from the river was highly suspect. Dysentery broke out at once and presented me with great problems. We opened a large War Hospital in the Sheik of Mohammerah's palace and I soon found myself as a patient, though assisting as a doctor as well. I recorded in my diary that it was well supplied with comforts from the Red Cross, including lovely pyjamas which I reluctantly gave up when I left!

Before the arrival of our main Mess stores by ship, our rationing was dull and monotonous. Our Colonel, a rather querulous man with a small body and surprisingly long and erratic legs, whose digestion constantly plagued him and indirectly us, frequently complained about the constant fare of curried bully beef (to which there was for a long time little possible alternative). 'Spackman', he would say with a sour smile, 'do you call this a curry? I call it a stew!' I got tired of hearing this moan, so one day I arranged to have a special curry made for him compounded almost entirely of chillies mixed

6

with all the hottest ingredients obtainable in the bazaar, to which we added hot chutney! The Colonel proceeded liberally to sprinkle this concoction with Tabasco sauce and then set about it. To his credit, he bravely managed to consume most of this fiendish dish and even commended it, albeit with suppressed gasps, draughts of water and much mopping of his brow! He never asked for a special curry again!

The problem of potable drinking water now became very pressing. There was quite an epidemic of dysentery amongst our Pioneers who were constantly occupied, when not fighting, with making roads, bridges and ramps. Water for all purposes had to be drawn from the river and this meant that, in practice, it was collected from the muddy tidal river bank, where it was more polluted than would be the case further out.

Sitting at ease on the flat roof of our billet, with air like that of a summer's evening at home, the view of the river only 100 yards away tempted me to consider how I could combine business with pleasure by getting hold of some sort of boat in which to go out among our transports and warships and return with bucket loads of water, which in anticipation, we imagined would be as clear and sparkling as it appeared to be in the evening light. So, following up this brainwave, I persuaded one of our officers, an acknowledged oarsman, to embark in a medium-sized native boat loaded with empty kerosene tins with me and three sepoys. We then made two or three successful trips at slack water, though the time consumed was rather excessive for the amount of rather dubiously coloured water obtained.

The success of this venture led to some possibly evilly disposed person in the Mess suggesting that I used a larger boat. I fell for this and 'borrowed' a small but rather unwieldy iron barge. The sepoys loved this sort of expedition as a welcome change from fatigues and drill and so off I went with a cheerful, but seriously inept, crew. We navigated out into a gentle current in promising style, but found that a strong ebb tide was running as we went further out. The infernal barge had no means of steering and my crew, like myself, though full of energy and goodwill, were all very inexperienced watermen, with the result that in a short time we were drifting broadside-on, downstream, at an ever gathering pace, out of control midst the river traffic! We crashed resoundingly against a couple of buoyed lighters and then fouled several anchor chains, leaving us in great risk of capsizing. Getting clear of these hazards we were alarmed to find a river steamer bearing down upon us, hooting furiously. Providentially, at this moment a steam launch appeared and, in the nick of time, hooked us up and towed us back to the bank and safety. All we had to show for our efforts was one 4-gallon tin of water and the Colonel, cautious at the best of times, expressed severe displeasure at the affair, poor little man. However, a gallant Sapper friend of mine, Matthews, solved the problem by rigging up a pump on a barge anchored in mid-stream and connecting it to a water tank on shore. Thereafter we were able to draw water without risking our lives from drowning. Naturally, I claimed the credit for engineering this development!

Chapter Two

Qurna – The Garden of Eden

A fortnight after we had captured Basra, our troops took Qurna, some thirty miles up river. It was, we were told, quite a brilliant affair but as we were still held in Basra carrying out pioneering jobs, I cannot describe it from personal observation. We went up soon after by the river steamer *Mejidieh*. It was our first trip on this hard-worked paddle boat and it was also our first meeting with the gallant Charlie Cowley, her skipper, who later gained the Victoria Cross and was shot in cold blood when captured by the Turks in his brave attempt to run a supply ship to us when we were beleaguered in Kut.

Qurna was locally reputed to be the site of the Garden of Eden, and although in winter the climate was at least tolerable, and justified Adam and Eve dressing up a bit, there were times in summer when one was not a bit surprised that they had left the place! A British Corporal succinctly expressed his opinion when he said (in rather more forthright language) 'Well, if this is the Garden of Eden, the bleeding angel wouldn't have needed a f---ing sword to keep me out!'

Naturally, local features gained Biblical names, such as Adam's Walk, Temptation Square, Serpent Alley, Rib Road, Apple Tree Yard, Eve's Garden and so on.

I myself nearly came to an unpleasant end the very first night we were there. We had just taken over the left flank of a perimeter camp facing north across the point of land between the Rivers Tigris and Euphrates (which form a confluence at Qurna) and had been told that the Arab village on our left towards the Euphrates was 'friendly'. How green we were to believe that statement! Like many others, I had found the river water did not agree with me and in the night I had to leave my small tent to obey the call of nature. I thought I knew where the latrine was, as I had previously fixed its position but, despite the bright moonlight, I failed to find it and spent some time wandering around in search of it. I then noticed two or three dim figures moving in the direction of the village and realized that they were the Arabs who had just crept into camp and stolen the latrine tent! So I scratched a hole in the sand and was just about to return to my tent when several shots were fired at me from the direction in which the Arabs had gone which only narrowly missed me! I made record time back to camp as a regular hullabaloo of yells and shouts, followed by more firing, commenced. As I hurriedly adjusted my clothes in my tent, a bullet struck one of the tent poles, bringing down the tent and adding to my confusion. This whole episode was treated with unseemly hilarity by my fellow officers, though sadly one of our Regimental shoemakers was killed, two sepoys wounded and one raiding Arab bayoneted in our trenches while trying to escape.

I managed to solve the everlasting water shortage here by digging a well and fixing a hand pump and hose line to it. I recorded in my diary that 'it was a great success and the water was pronounced delicious, in spite of the number of ancient bones and skulls we had dug out of the well!'

At this time a bridge of boats was made across the Tigris and a high observation tower built above the palm trees from which, in the distance, we could see smoke from the Turkish vessels far up the river. There was at this time little or no fighting of a serious nature but we had some fun with the Arabs who had a habit of making demonstrations by firing their guns at a safe distance, on foot or horseback, and by displaying flags. They may have been trying to locate our guns, and in this they succeeded for it became a regular evening amusement for the guns to have a go at them. I doubt the guns hit anything of significance but it helped to pass the time. At night the Arabs would creep up closer and snipe at the camp. When this became too much of a nuisance the Gunners would fire off a few star shells to light up the foreground to give our riflemen a chance to get their own back.

As we seemed to be stuck at Qurna for some time, I bought for the Mess a charming little milch cow for £5. It had a gay little calf that went quite mad after each feed. She was taken on our strength for ration purposes (posing as a mule!) and she 'gave us milk with all her might' for many a long day, making river trips, still as a 'mule', on steamers and barges until the bad days when we had no animals of any sort left. The sepoys looked after her with delight as she reminded them of their own village life in India.

Even with these diversions time was inclined to hang and, in order to keep ourselves and the sepoys interested, we made up parties to travel up the Euphrates in bellums hunting snipe and wild pig. The Colonel viewed these excursions with his usual doubt and suspicion but was finally persuaded on Major Riddell's advice to sanction them, albeit with reluctance, on the grounds that it was desirable to train the men in the handling of river craft. This turned out to be a sensible precaution later. We occasionally got sniped at by marsh Arabs from among the reeds, but we always had with us at least one bellum crew armed with service rifles to provide covering fire. It must be admitted that when a pig was sighted there was more danger to life from the fire of the excited sepoys than from the occasional Arab lurking in the palm groves! These wild pig were numerous and of great size. On one occasion, I landed on a sand bank looking for snipe while the others were chasing pig only to find a huge old boar charging in my direction on my island of sand. He turned away at the last minute, but the rest of the party displayed great hilarity over the way I danced about facing him with my shot gun, which was only loaded with No 9 shot, fit only for bringing down snipe! Pig could swim very fast and galloped at high speed on firm ground, but floundered in an ungainly manner in shallow water or soft mud, when they became easier targets. When killed they were loaded in triumph into the bellums and provided a feast of pork back in camp.

11

What a strange contrast our campaign presented at this time with the war being waged in Flanders where the British and French Armies were locked in a grim struggle with the German Armies in cold, muddy trenches, suffering continual bombardment from massed artillery. I knew that two of my brothers (Charles and Maurice) were in Flanders and I felt for their plight. Here in 'Mespots' we were engaged in a real old-fashioned war of movement with periods of savage open fighting, alternating with periods of tranquillity, upon and besides the great Rivers Tigris and Euphrates.

Looking back, despite what was to follow, I think that on balance we had the best of it compared with Flanders.

Chapter Three

Shaiba, April 1915

In Qurna while the waters of the old River Tigris were flowing peacefully past us down to the sea at Basra, the Turks were not idle. Their reaction to our initial advance was to attempt to interrupt the oil pipeline leading from the Persian oilfields and even to try to reach the terminal oil refinery at Abadan, below Basra.

An even more serious threat to our main base at Basra was the launching by them of a strong force along the western side, bypassing Qurna down the main River Euphrates channel from Nasiriya. The Turks had already established an advance position not far from Shaiba, only eighteen miles west of Basra across low-lying open desert. Our political officers were worried at the adverse effect this force was having on the allegiance of both the nomadic and settled Arabs in the area of Zobair and down as far as Kuwait. Kuwait was not then famous, oil not yet having been discovered in the Sheik's territory.

To counter these threats, in March we were moved down to Basra to a camp in a palm grove on the edge of the plain, across which came sweeping a scorching dusty wind. By April the heat was terrible, with a shade temperature up to 120 degrees F (40 degrees C) day after day. There was no shade for the fighting troops, the only relief being occasional violent dust storms which ended up in torrential downpours of rain, turning the dust into mud.

Fresh regiments and line reinforcements were now arriving from India, including a heavy battery of 5-inch guns drawn along in stately fashion by teams of splendid, huge bullocks, white and placid, ignorant of the sad fate awaiting them at Kut a year later. A Territorial Battalion of the Hampshire Regiment soon arrived bringing their band which played popular selections on Sunday evenings. Life that March began to assume the routine of an Indian cantonment.

I can remember one Sunday when two officers and I loaded our tiffin and some beer in a bellum crewed by Arab watermen and set off down river for a picnic, after calling in at the hospital to enquire about some of our Regiment's sick soldiers. We rowed up a very pretty creek lined with fruit gardens and orange groves. There were pomegranates, figs, date palms and flowering shrubs, making it a popular resort for the local young people on a Sunday afternoon. I recorded the scene in my diary as follows:

> We tied up to the bank and after tiffin gave away the remaining cakes to a small and very bashful Arab maiden aged about five by calling out 'tai, tal, tai' (sweets, come here, sweets). She soon disposed of these, aided by other small infants in the background and then came creeping back for more.
>
> We continued up the creek coming upon a group of about twenty young town Arabs who were having a picnic in their best clothes, sitting in a circle on the ground and making a great noise. Some had small drums which they beat with their hands; the others were clapping their hands and snapping their fingers. To this accompaniment they sang a sad dirge and some did a shuffling dance within the circle. At the chorus they all jumped up and danced, stamping violently and shouting three times before subsiding to the ground again.
>
> Finally a huge basket of food was produced and, in return for our giving them some beer, they offered us some small glasses of sweet tea, without milk, which we drank with appropriate gestures of salutation.
>
> On our return journey, we passed many bellums full of the youth and beauty of the town. There were parties of girls in

bellums, wearing their finest, most highly coloured clothes and adorned with makeup, plaited hair, and red flowers behind their ears, bangles, earrings and necklaces. With their Arab features and olive complexions the girls looked very attractive and soon drew similar boat loads of young men to the gardens to exchange flowers, compliments, badinage, laughter and songs, followed by picnics.

In addition to my role as Medical Officer to the Regiment, I was responsible for running the Officers' Mess. I built a fly-proof cookhouse but nevertheless had to submit to some complaints, notably from the Colonel, usually because of the difficulty of disguising the field rations. While awaiting further action, I bought two geese to fatten up for the Mess. Almost immediately one was stolen, so we ate the other promptly! Our tough little Mess cook survived not only the hardships of a long and arduous campaign, followed by the rigors of the siege of Kut, but he even survived both the long march north and the long periods of captivity in the prison camps of Anatolia.

News from Shaiba was not encouraging and daily we heard gunfire from that direction. It was a relief when we received orders to march to Shaiba on 5 April 1915. It turned out to be a difficult march, only eighteen miles in all, but with much of it through the flooded countryside, with water up to one's knees and only bellums for transport. About every mile there might be a small sand island suitable for a halt. I was in charge of the rearguard and was provided with some mules to collect up those falling by the wayside. Our sepoys marched barefoot in contrast to a British Regiment whose men wore boots and consequently found the going very exhausting. I soon found my mules fully laden and had to heliograph ahead for assistance after which we were sent two spare bellums and some more mules. Our sepoys were magnificent and, as they marched off the last island of sand, they raised their Sikh war cry, earning the congratulations of our Brigadier General Fry who was watching the arrival from the far shore. At that stage we still had four miles to go to our allotted position and we finally arrived after dark with a sandstorm blowing up.

15

This sandstorm was sheer hell. It blew all that night and all the next day. Our little tents were quite useless, cooking and eating was impossible, so that I spent most of the day sitting on the sand with my Burberry over my head, eyes red and throat and lungs all choked up. All military activity was suspended on both sides.

While waiting for the forthcoming battle, we worked hard on the defensive position in anticipation of a Turkish attack. They were doing the same ten miles away but were in greater strength than we were and, in addition, had a not entirely reliable Arab force in the background, a sort of irregular cavalry, more concerned with pillage than in formal fighting. I little knew that my personal introduction to the serious business of close quarter combat was imminent.

Unexpectedly, at dawn on 12 April, I was awakened by a fusillade of rifle and machine-gun fire coming from the plain in front. Our outposts came in unscathed, according to plan, after firing a few rounds, withdrawing to inside our wire. I went at once to our trenches to join the sepoys and sat down beside one of the machine-gunners. Looking out, I saw a line of Turks advancing in extended order in several echelons, with massed supporting infantry following up behind. Simultaneously the enemy guns opened up on us, shelling the old fort just behind the trenches, with the result that we received a lot of 'short' artillery rounds in addition to the heavy rifle fire. The noise was simply deafening, especially when our own guns then opened up. I felt seriously tensed-up but could not tear myself away from the action. It was more than I could bear to stand there doing nothing, so I seized a rifle from a sepoy, loaded a clip of rounds and gave the Turks a burst of rapid fire, remembering first to tear off the Red Cross brassard from my arm! After that gesture of defiance, and with my morale restored, I returned the rifle to its grinning owner and replaced my brassard.

Shortly after this an officer named Farebrother of the Norfolk Regiment, accompanied by two Tommy's, was hit by a shell when dragging ammunition across an exposed gap on our position. I rushed to my covered dressing station for a stretcher party and, guided by the Company Commander, Major Riddell, went out to collect them. It wasn't exactly healthy for, although the rifle fire had died down, salvoes of shells were still falling. Riddell was as cool under fire as on parade. Sadly this gallant and brilliant officer was tragically killed in action only six months later. We got poor Farebrother onto a stretcher and back to the comparative safety of my dressing station. He had been shot through the spine, poor devil, and was paralysed and in agony. He told me he wished he had been killed outright. All I could do was to give him a shot of morphine and a cigarette. The Field Ambulance, to which we back-loaded casualties after first aid had been administered, was located in the fort just behind us but the snag was that the Turks had some snipers covering the open ground leading from our position to it and they could also cover the Great Door leading into it. We had to make several trips carrying wounded up to this door and occasionally a bullet would smack into the mud wall of the fort while we scurried towards it, not bothering to 'break step' as stretcher bearers are required to do by field regulations! Farebrother was in due course evacuated to Basra but I did not hear if he survived.

During the afternoon the Turks renewed their attack, advancing boldly and gallantly despite heavy losses. We were dug in, in good defensive trenches and suffered few casualties. My stretcher bearers had been splendid throughout and so I recommended two of them for the gallantry award, Mention in Dispatches. During this campaign no one was ever granted leave but you might qualify for a trip back to India if severely wounded or seriously ill.

That night was very unpleasant as the Turks kept creeping up to try to cut our barbed wire, throwing in bombs for good measure. So we lit up the foreground with star shells keeping them at bay but we got little sleep. By dawn they had returned to their shallow trenches about half a mile away. There they were given no peace as our guns bombarded them and, although they fired at us briskly at first, shortage of ammunition and lack of water and food under the burning sun reduced their activity considerably. My comment at the time seems now, fifty years later [ed. revised by WCS in 1965], callous, and unfair to these gallant Turkish soldiers:

One of the Norfolk Regiment's machine gunners was quickly on to every man who left the comparative safety of the trench to double back, dodging this way and that, but the marksman usually got him in three or four shots. I was in the trenches all the morning when our best shots were ordered to snipe at them whenever a head was seen above the parapet or someone tried to go to the rear from the trenches. It was most thrilling.

The Turks in this particular trench, at about noon that day, waved a white flag and, when we ceased firing, about 120 men stood up from what appeared to be quite a small trench. We sent out an armed party and took them all prisoner. They were from a crack Constantinople regiment. I knew that there must be a number of Turkish soldiers lying wounded out in the burning sand so I got permission to take out a stretcher party to rescue them. Protection was provided by a platoon from our Regiment under Major H.J. Riddell and a Company officer, 2nd Lieutenant Venis. We had not gone far across the sandbanks in that area when we came under fire from enemy trenches on our right flank. Almost at once my colleague, the MO of a British Regiment, was killed close by and a few men wounded. Major Riddell immediately led his sepoys forward in attack, whilst my small detachment formed a second line, firing to cover his advance and dashing forward when his men were in firing positions. By this time we were amongst the sand dunes and out of sight of our own lines. To add to our discomfort one of our own batteries back in the main Shaiba position mistook us for Turks and landed a salvo near us. It was terrifying for a while until the brave Major Riddell stood up and waved his topi above his head, which unmilitary sign was quickly seen and recognized by the Gunner forward observer, who ceased firing. We then rushed the Turkish trench, the occupants of which promptly surrendered. Our casualties in this minor skirmish were two killed and seven wounded. I gave the wounded treatment and then had the opportunity of watching a bayonet charge of the 24th Punjabis onto another nearby Turkish trench. This was a most exciting period, particularly as we were rushing forward right behind the sepoys. In the aftermath, the wounded of both sides, along with captured rifles and ammunition, were loaded onto mule carts and sent to the rear in a column with two captured cannon and 370 prisoners. 'Quite something to show' was the comment in my diary.

This overture to the Battle of Shaiba turned out to be a sort of 'home and away' fixture. They attacked us on 12 April. On 13 April we drove them off and the Divisional staff prepared for a major attack onto the strong main Turkish defensive position, in the uncomfortable knowledge that a large body of irregular and bloodthirsty mounted Arabs were hovering like vultures on the edge of the battlefield, waiting to fall on the hapless losers, whichever side that might be.

The very next day the Division advanced in widely extended line across the flat, shimmering desert, in burning sunshine, leaving our Regiment as rearguard after our exertions of the previous day. This is how I described the ensuing battle, the Battle of Shaiba, when I found time to write-up my diary two days later:

Our troops passed slowly over the horizon and into the sand-dunes, disappearing into the dust, accompanied by a continuous roar of artillery and musket fire as battle was joined. It was not long before the wounded and stragglers began to return. It was a fearfully hot, scorching morning and the well in our position was soon surrounded by exhausted men and gallant 'bhisties' (the true Gunga Dins), who having refilled their water-skins trudged back towards the battle with them slung over their backs.

The wounded men told us of heavy losses suffered from the well-concealed enemy position, which was supported by skilfully-handled machine guns. Our anxiety increased every hour as no progress was being made, and, at 1500 hrs we received an urgent message to go forward in order to cover the withdrawal of our Brigades, taking all available transport with us to bring in the wounded and dead.

When we had traversed the low crest ahead of our position, the enemy mistook our long column, enveloped in dust, for heavy reinforcements of fresh troops and their resistance finally collapsed, the attack being completed with a bayonet charge. Their forces had been much more seriously weakened than we knew at the time and withdrawal had even been contemplated. They subsequently abandoned their main camp in Barjisiya Wood, retreating north pell-mell, whilst being mercilessly harried by their erstwhile allies, the treacherous Arabs.

We recovered all the wounded and most of the dead that night, total casualties being 1,200 men. A number of my friends were killed, alas. Some were riddled with bullets, sustaining fearful injuries, enough to horrify even a doctor. The Turks were reported to have fought most tenaciously. Their Divisional Commander was killed but they managed to get nearly all their guns away, including some howitzers manned by German crews.

The day after a big battle is the worst of all days. You hear which of your friends have been killed, see the lines of dead laid out and treat the wounded patiently waiting for attention to their terrible injuries. I went to the main hospital and worked all day, first sorting wounded for casualty evacuation back to Basra in a convoy, and then putting on dressings. Towards evening I moved into the 'operating theatre' (a tent), the surgeons being exhausted, where I performed operations on a number of compound fractures and other tasks until 2100 hrs, fixing them up ready, as far as was possible, for transport by bellum convoy to Basra next day.

Pause to imagine being brought in, with other wounded with broken limbs or massive injuries, on a mule cart without springs, travelling for miles across the rough desert under a burning sun. Imagine the pain and the thirst. That evening cartloads of dead and wounded Turks were brought in, the dead, dying and wounded all mixed up, the job of sorting them out being an appalling experience. No, there is nothing romantic, picturesque or glorious about the aftermath of a battle, with the maimed and wounded dying before your helpless eyes. Picture the squalor and the despair of the tired and overworked nursing staff struggling to give proper attention to each case. Such an experience is something to have seen, but then to try to forget.

The Indian Supply and Transport Corps claimed that they won the Battle of Shaiba with their column of AT carts (see above) being mistaken for fresh troops and artillery, and indeed this is acknowledged in the Official History, but there are times when officialdom becomes the enemy of efficiency, as the following incident shows. In clearing up after the battle one of my tasks was to supervise the loading and dispatch of a bellum convoy across the flood water to Basra and on to the base hospitals in order that the overcrowded and overworked Field Ambulances in Shaiba Fort could be cleared and made ready for any imminent local needs. It was essential that the convoy should get away by a certain hour, about noon, in order to reach safety on the other side before nightfall, because the whole area was infested with fierce but cowardly Arab horsemen looking for an opportunity to prey upon parties unable effectively to protect themselves. The sick and wounded were, therefore, moved up to the water's edge from the Field Ambulances where I and my helpers, working against time, set about loading them onto the bellums, wading deep into the water, carrying stretcher cases. My instructions were to keep a nominal roll of all casualties sent on the convoy.

As the evening began to close in, the officer in charge of the convoy eventually insisted that it must leave, which left me in a dilemma. I could either get those remaining on the bank loaded, counted and dispatched, but without a completed nominal roll or, as an alternative, complete the paperwork of those loaded but retain some twenty poor souls still undocumented and on the bank and send them back to the Field Ambulance to await passage the next day. I decided it was more humane to get them away, and we did so, in the nick of time. As the convoy left, the Commanding Officer of the Field ambulance rode up on his horse, a glittering figure.

'Well, Spackman,' he said, 'have they all got away?'

'Yes Sir' I replied, wiping the sweat from my brow.

'Well done! Give me the nominal rolls'

I then had to explain that although we had a record of the total number sent off, I had an incomplete nominal roll. I proposed that a signal be sent to Basra giving the total number dispatched and the number of bellums sent, asking that nominal rolls be completed on arrival, if deemed necessary. Shock, amazement and horror! The Colonel, a veteran of the South African War, and a stickler for regulations, was so shocked that he nearly fell off his horse. On recovering, I received a major dressing down, not a comfortable experience, as junior officers were at that time in considerable awe of senior field officers.

It is a sad reflection on this slavish observance of field regulations that the only DSO awarded to any Medical Officer during the Shaiba operations was given to an officer who remained on the Basra side of the waters during the battle but who had meticulously set up his hospital according to the rules!

Two days after the battle ended, I accompanied some troops at dawn across the battlefield to the Barjisiya Wood where the Turks had their HQ. Most of the Turkish dead were lying where they had fallen, a pitiful sight, and highly unpleasant too. One large trench, which had been taken by a bayonet charge, held about 200 bodies. The ground behind that trench back to the wood was also dotted with bodies. I then found the Turkish field hospital, which was in a shocking mess with dead and wounded still lying there. I did what I could for the wounded and took them back in mule carts. The dreaded Arabs had already been in and had looted everything of value.

On another day I rode over the desert to the Arab town of Zobair and met the Sheik (Ibrahim) who was friendly to the British. An extract from my diary gives a picture of life in a local village that time:

Zobair pleased me very much, a nice orderly town fully walled and with city gates huge and studded with iron through which the women came out to draw water in copper jars from the great well, quite biblical. A fine open space was used as a market, full of camels, donkeys and trading Arabs. There were piles of melons, for which this district is famous, and a gunsmith's shop stocked with primitive weapons, side by side with cheap modern revolvers made in Birmingham!

22

There was a shady wall along one side of the market square with a broad ledge along it about four feet above the ground and with steps up to it. It was fitted with a long coir mat and oriental carpets. Seated on this, with a few of his intimates, the Sheik kept an eye on everything while the marketing was at its busiest and before the heat became too oppressive. Here he heard disputes and received petitions. Furthermore he could watch the young women walking gracefully, with water pots on their heads, to and from the well. How could a Sheik spend a more pleasant and profitable hour whilst having his morning glass of coffee? On my visit I was accompanied by Colonel Smyth of the Political Department, and a cavalry escort, and we met the Sheik, a fine looking man with a hawk-like nose, and his sons. They made a picturesque group for my camera against the background of the arched gateway.

Chapter Four

Townshend's Regatta

As a direct result of the Battle of Shaiba, which was a real old fashioned soldiers' battle of dour slogging tactics, the Turks had retreated in confusion up the Euphrates to Nasiriyeh and the High Command had to decide whether to hold the country only up to as far as Qurna or to advance further up the Tigris. As this is a personal narrative I am not going to discuss the pros and cons but merely say that the fighting troops were delighted at the decision, which was taken by some unknown higher authority, to press on up the Tigris. This determination to make a major advance led at once to the exciting and colourful affair known as 'Townshend's Regatta'. This name arose from the fact that our GOC was now Major General Townshend and the whole operation had to be carried out across a flooded landscape.

Major General Townshend, with a reputation of being a brilliant and ambitious tactician, had just arrived to take command of our 6th (Indian) Division and, at the time, we entered into the spirit of the game with great enthusiasm and little or no thought of the perils which might beset us. In preparation for the advance, we returned across the floods to Basra to reorganize. The waters were even deeper, reaching in places to the girths of our horses, while the sepoys had to march with their boots slung around their necks. It took six hours to cross six miles of the floodwater which was quite choppy, churned up by the 'shamaal' wind which was now blowing.

Soon after we had settled in to our riverside camp, spring tides at full moon, combined with strong winds, caused floods to breach the bund around the camp in several places and we were inundated with rushing water. Our Pioneers, despite violent thunderstorms in the night, desperately worked to save part of the area and managed to secure the hospitals and other vital areas but we were amused to see the Brigadier's tent was under two feet of water. On the whole the inconvenience was slight. The unmetalled roads were adequate, as we had no need to move artillery batteries and we had no airstrip as we had no aircraft! Our reconnaissance was done by the cavalry. The whole of lower Mesopotamia up to thirty miles north of Qurna was under flood at that time of year, due to the great rivers being swelled by melting snow in the Kurdish mountains far to the north. The worst affected region lay between the two great rivers and here the Turks could only defend dry islands and ridges amongst the reedy marshes. Here it was easy to get lost in the intricate pattern of channels and to become prey to the hostile marsh Arabs who moved in light 'mashoofs' (coracles) made of woven reeds daubed with pitch.

The main river was our principal highway and up it went a large and varied armada carrying troops, guns, ammunition and all the supplies needed for the move forward. In addition to three or four Tigris paddle steamers, various warships of the Royal Navy and Indian Marine, tugs and launches, we had been reinforced with half a dozen paddle steamers from the Irrawaddy River, Burma, which arrived after a perilous sea journey across the Indian Ocean, during which passage at least one foundered in a storm. There was also one patriotic but eccentric planter, Chalmers, from Assam, who had insisted on being towed across in a sort of houseboat called *Aerial* which drew only eighteen inches of water and was powered by an aeroplane propeller! It was rather like a prototype hovercraft and came in useful on many occasions because he could get up speed and get right alongside the shore. Like a hovercraft it had difficulty in steering in strong wind or current.

Preparations for the 'Regatta' then began in earnest. The paddle steamers were now loaded with the field guns and had huge iron barges, for stores, attached alongside each side of the ship. There were hundreds of bellums, each capable of carrying eight soldiers or sepoys, and the Sappers had made protective iron shields with loopholes for many of them. Very comic looking! Our sepoys showed great enthusiasm when learning to paddle or punt them along, occasioning much shouting, laughing and splashing. The boats were organized into four columns, identified by coloured flags. My column was Green column.

We travelled up to our advanced base Qurna on the *Mejidieh*, with Captain Charley Cowley in charge, a field gun mounted on the foredeck and with our little brown cow amongst the mules on the barge alongside. During the journey we were thrilled to see a small biplane flying overhead making its first flight over the enemy's position on the first day of the Regatta! However it soon developed engine trouble, whilst the two seaplanes we had were never even able to get airborne.

At Qurna the weather was terribly hot, with almost 100 per cent humidity. When making the least physical effort, my khaki cotton shirt became black with sweat just as if I had fallen in the river. Down in Basra there were a number of deaths from heat-stroke but strange to say none occurred in the forward area during the excitement of Townshend's Regatta.

So, on 31 May 1915, the great advance commenced and we moved forward in the dawn, with high morale and eager to get on with the task in hand after a good rest since the Battle of Shaiba. The grumbles about quarters, the climate and the short-comings of rations were forgotten and, surprise, surprise, the sick in hospital made rapid recoveries and applied to rejoin their units! How different was our picturesque and relatively uncomplicated campaign in Mesopotamia compared with the squalor, drabness and frightful mass slaughter of the campaign in progress in Flanders.

When the advance began our guns opened up and the Turks returned our fire, while we in our bellums worked our way forward in and out of the high reeds. As we reached each small defensive position, given names such as One Tree Hill, Gun Hill, Norfolk Island, the Turks drew back as best they could before we reached them. Every piece of firm ground was of tactical significance. The river channel was marked above the floods by an irregular line of palm trees. The channel was said to be mined, which turned out to be a false alarm, and was obstructed at one point by two sunken barges, nicknamed Erna and Emma, which were soon blown up, poor dears!

An exhilarating running fight ensued as we pursued the Turks up the winding river, past Ezra's Tomb standing on the right bank, a dilapidated structure with a stumpy minaret of yellow brick, decked out with patterns and mosaics, quite a landmark in the featureless landscape. In order to escape capture, the crews of the Turkish ships jettisoned their barges and mahelas loaded with supplies, ammunition and even troops. Their only warship, the sloop *Marmaris*, ran aground and was set on fire, the smoke being visible to us still in our bellums in the reeds. Our flagship, the *Espiegle*, had to turn back here, the river becoming too shallow for her, but our armed tugs pressed on up the river relentlessly all that day and the next, far out-distancing the slow-moving paddleboats towing the barges filled with the impatient troops.

This unplanned enterprise by the armed tugs led to the capture of Amara on 2 June, a daring and spectacular affair. Amara was an important, well-built town on the left bank of the River Tigris, with good wharves and warehouses supporting a thriving caravan route into Persia (Iran). It also had a bridge made of boats, the only one between Baghdad and the Persian Gulf, the centre section of which could be swung aside to allow the passage of river steamers. The right bank was where the wealthy Arab merchants had houses with well-irrigated gardens. The enterprise began when Lieutenant Commander Singleton RN, commanding the armed tug *Shaitan* (Satan), manned by eight ratings and accompanied by a motor launch with two Marines, somewhat foolhardily set off in full pursuit of the Turks who were fleeing in what had become a rout. They were closely followed by the armed yacht *Comet*, carrying no less a person than the dynamic General Townshend himself, with an escort of twelve soldiers. Entering a straight stretch of river they found that they were entering Amara itself, which was still full of Turkish troops milling about in panic and confusion, alarmed at being at the mercy of the Arab hordes if they retreated in disorder. For after their grim experiences at Shaiba, the Turks knew that they would receive brutal treatment from the Arab irregulars if they did not keep together.

As the *Shaitan* steamed against a strong current towards the town, she fired a couple of shots which resulted, to their alarm, in 100 armed Turks pouring out of the coffee shops. However, instead of offering resistance, they piled their arms and indicated readiness to surrender. They were ordered through an interpreter on the bridge of the tug to march alongside the tug on the quayside, collecting more and more troops from other coffee shops till a whole battalion had surrendered! They were told that a large British force had arrived. In this remarkable coup, the whole of Amara was captured, without resistance, by only a handful of men, and what is more no main body of troops reached the town until two days later. At the time of surrender the nearest effective infantry force was still on river steamers many miles downstream.

Meanwhile, an additional tug and launch joined the *Shaitan* and *Comet*, making a total compliment of twenty-nine naval ratings and marines and twelve soldiers, to hold the entire town, which still contained large numbers of Turkish and Arab troops. The situation was eased by the arrival of the Norfolks two days later on 4 June but by then the central barracks, occupied by a battalion of regular Turkish troops, had surrendered to a naval lieutenant, accompanied by one sailor and one marine. In all, nearly 2,000 prisoners were taken, together with great quantities of stores of all kinds. It is hardly surprising that the troops began to believe that they were invincible!

While all these exciting events were happening up ahead of us in Amara, our war bellums were struggling on at best speed among the reedy marshes. I was with a company of the 48th Pioneers under Major Riddell, with 2nd Lieutenant Venis as his subaltern, with orders to capture a small Turkish position called Mezeebla, near Ezra's Tomb. It was nothing more than a sand-bank about a mile long and a few feet above sea level. Our local Arab guide seemed a bit scared, as well he might be, and we wondered if he would try to get us lost among the intersecting channels which were hemmed in by a mass of towering reeds. As a precaution, a sepoy kept a rifle muzzle pressed against the guide's ribs! There was always the chance of an ambush by hostile Muntafiq Arabs infiltrating the reeds in their canoes but we emerged safely and without incident into open water, with Mezeeba straight ahead. Our warlike Sikhs were then disappointed to find that the Turks had already withdrawn from the objective. We found the island in a terrible state of squalor, with millions of flies, mosquitoes and sandflies, and an intolerable stench pervading the air from some hastily and inadequately buried bodies. The sandbank was without vegetation and the heat and humidity made life on it almost unbearable. Even the most enthusiastic travel agent would have found it difficult to recommend a stay in the area! Another hazard was dodging occasional shots fired from the reeds by Arabs, causing us to dig in rapidly. We were pretty uncomfortable as we carried only light bivouac tents, the Mess cook was way back on the steamer with the battalion and my servant, carrying only bare rations, was a poor substitute.

The nights were particularly trying. Because of a slight fall in temperature, the humidity increased. The sandflies were so small that they could get in through a mosquito net. You could not hear them buzz, and they could not be seen by the light of a hurricane lamp. Their sting was the most irritating of all such stings, to say nothing of the chance of developing sandfly fever. It was far too hot to try to protect yourself with even a thin cotton sheet so I spent most of that night lying uncomfortably in the shallow waters of the shelving river bank, risking taking a mouthful of dirty Tigris water if I dozed off. Next night I gave up any idea of repeating this procedure when I heard that one of our sepoys had gone fishing with a baited hook and caught a shark!

Needless to say such trivialities did not worry that imperturbable professional soldier par excellence Major Riddell, who was a bachelor. Despite this, he had a surprisingly romantic streak in his make-up which came out at this time. Wherever he went he always carried with him a copy of the *Oxford Book of Victorian Verse*, printed on thin India paper and on this desolate

29

strand, doubtless depressed at being left behind away from the excitements of the main advance, he read to young Venis and me some of his favourite passages. I have this book beside me now. I acquired it after Riddell was killed and it was the only book I was able to carry with me wherever I travelled, even as a prisoner of war. It bears the Turkish censor's stamp and my name and rank inscribed (upside down) in Arabic script, as well as Riddell's signature.

To console us as we sat between the sun and the moon on the yellow sand upon the shore he recited from memory much of Tennyson's *Lotus Eaters*, with its glorious rhythms. Certainly there was nothing to make us wish to tarry there and we were happy to be called forward; Riddell's company for fighting and field work up the Euphrates (where many of his men were killed), and I to Amara to join the rest of the battalion of Sikhs and Jats. I was picked up by a crazy little stern-wheeler, the *Muzaffari*, which had, in its early service, taken part in the expedition which set out to relieve General Gordon, besieged in Khartoum in 1884.

The journey to Amara was a delightful experience of which I have vivid memories. There were three or four other officers on board, adequate food and drink and just enough room on deck for us to relax, playing some good records of grand opera, captured from the Germans in Basra, on an old horn gramophone. The little steamer struggled gamely against the fluctuating current, often so unsuccessfully that it took an hour to round a tricky bend in the river. However we hadn't a care in the world! The steam boiler kept breaking down and our little engineer, of mixed parentage, grimy and cheerful, kept tearing off strips of his clothing to bind up leaks in the steam pipe, so that by the time we got to Amara the legs of his trousers were of different lengths! He was a merry little man and we rewarded him well.

Amara was a pleasant town in which to be temporarily stationed. The river level had fallen and the climate was less humid, though the day temperature still reached 100 degrees F daily. The Jahala canal, north of the town, provided a popular bathing place for the British troops, well away from view of the

30

ladies. There was a good open market, well supplied with fruit, poultry and fresh vegetables to give much needed variety to Mess meals. Eggs were three pence a dozen (not always fresh), chickens at four pence each and milk at two pence a quart.

Colourful caravans arrived almost daily from Luristan, Kurdistan and the remoter East, via the Pusht-i-Kuh mountains, bearing merchandise on their jingling camels and mules along the traditional trade routes leading away along the Silk Road into Central Asia, Bokhara and Samarkand. Such caravans had passed this way for centuries, to and fro, harried on certain stretches by brigands or hostile tribes. They saw no reason to be deterred from their ancient and profitable trade by a mere conflict between the Western Powers.

It was an unforgettable experience to stand in the wide open market square at the time of arrival or departure of a caravan, hearing the low-pitched jingle of mule bells, the disgruntled bubbling of the camels and the Babel of human tongues; and to admire the strange clothes and the outlandish hats of felt or fur of the merchants and their servants, all with formidable daggers tucked into their voluminous belts. Persians, Kurds, Bakhtiaris and Lurs mingled and bargained with local Arabs, Jews, Armenians, Chaldeans, Sabeans and Greeks. There was even a sect of devil-worshippers, very worthy and cheerful characters. The market porters were Lurs and Bakhtiaris and they possessed fantastic carrying strength. We saw them staggering along under colossal crates and sacks held to their backs by bands of goat hair webbing which passed forward to their sweating foreheads.

The Sabeans, a sect of Christians, specialized in making silver-ware with inlaid designs of black enamel of a very attractive kind, similar to that made around Lake Van further north. The most famous artist in this work in Amara was one Zahroon. His tobacco boxes, ash trays and belt buckles were decorated with local scenes of dhows, palm trees and camels, surrounded by scrolls and elaborate script. He made me a silver beaker to my design and signed it with his name, 'Amara Zahroon', but sadly I was unable to safeguard it during the troubles which lay ahead.

31

The Turk has often confounded his opponents by his powers of recovery after an overwhelming disaster and this resilience was now about to be demonstrated in this campaign. The Turkish force we had defeated so soundly at Shaiba was soon reformed at Nasiriyeh, further up the Euphrates where, strengthened by reinforcements from Baghdad, it took up a strong position threatening our flank. We were consequently summoned from our comfortable quarters to proceed down river again to Qurna, preparatory to sailing up the Euphrates to join Major Riddell, whose company was already operating as part of the British force on that flank.

Chapter Five

Interlude up the Euphrates

On our return to Qurna we found it sadly quiet compared with the palmy days before the Regatta when it was bustling with military importance and amphibious activity. It now had a forgotten air, being only a minor stopping point on the lines of communication. There were no mules squealing in Apple Tree Yard and no local produce for sale in the market in Temptation Square. The only redeeming point was the splendid crop of ripe shining dates on the palms in Eve's Garden.

To reach the fighting on the Nasiriyeh front we sailed right-handed up the Euphrates channel into the Hammar Lake, a wide stretch of shallow water within the marshes between the two great rivers, Euphrates and Tigris. This lake was about four feet deep in April/May, falling in autumn to an area of mudflats and narrow channels connecting the Arab villages. When we arrived the water was rapidly falling and we were rarely free of the bottom and repeatedly got stuck. Our progress was only maintained by kedging and by sepoys wading and hauling the boats. While engaged in trying to make progress we could hear the sounds of the fighting waxing and waning in the far distance.

Finding slightly deeper water, we got a tug to take tow of one of our encumbered barges and so reached the bund which Major Riddell's company of Sikhs, supported by the Sappers, had blown up under the noses of the Turks. It was a great sadness to me that we had not arrived in time to dress our wounded, or to assist a brave Sikh officer of the 48th who had died of wounds.

This expedition was entirely dependent on water transport for the movement of equipment, stores and, in many cases, troops. The essential requirement for this transport was that of minimum draught. The Senior Naval Officer's flagship was another veteran craft, the *Shushan*, a stern-wheel paddle steamer, which had also taken part in the Khartoum operation, mounted in 1884 to go to the relief of General Gordon. Its companion was our old friend the *Muzzafari*, which had carried me from Mezeebla to Amara the month before. The same cheerful engineer greeted me and invited me to admire the polish on the vintage Maxim gun mounted on *Muzzafari's* foredeck.

We stayed for only one week near the blown up bund, the Turks having already been put to flight and the local population scattered. Although the ruins of Ur of the Chaldees were not far away, sightseeing was impossible as the urgent task was to pull back from the Nasiriyeh front so as to get the 'fleet' away before the Hammar Lake level fell further and imprisoned our ships until released by the advent of the flood water of the following spring. The Hammar Lake had now fallen to two feet six inches and the *Mosul*, the steamer we were embarked on, only made it back to Qurna and the Tigris by offloading everything possible into fleets of bellums. Sepoys, waist deep in water and mud, hauled and heaved on hawsers, towing the bellums in strings, while the crews, mostly Chaldeans, waded about seeking out the deep channels. If it had not been for the presence of these ancient stern-wheelers tugging barges, gun-flats and mahelas, I don't know how the expedition could possibly have extricated itself!

The military command had decided that it was imperative that the advance up the Tigris be pressed forward so we did not stop at Qurna but, after transferring to a great iron barge tied alongside a river steamer, started for Amara that same evening. We passed Mezeebla, much enlarged, without regret, then Ezra's Tomb, passing through little reed villages on the river banks and admiring the antics of the fair-haired Arab children splashing about in the water. On the third day we reached Amara once more and they were, as was reported in a contemporary military newsletter (*Truth*):

All fit as fighting cocks and pleased with the victorious little campaign going on out here, the only show where we seem to have the enemy fairly on the run.

These river trips were quite enjoyable despite the burning heat reflected from the bare iron decks of the barges. We tied up every night and bivouacked on the bank, usually getting some shooting at black partridge or sand grouse at dusk or dawn. The old river was always father and mother to us, our only source of water for all purposes. We could never move far from it and on its brown and placid surface it carried everything that would float, as it had done from the dawn of history, from the 'kelek' (a raft mentioned by Xenophon and still in use), the 'guffa' (round like a coracle and tricky to steer), mashoof, mahela and dhow, to the present day big river steamers.

The river steamers usually had a steel lighter tied to each side which slowed them up and which increased the danger of them running aground. Each would have an Arab with a long pole at the bow probing the water and singing out the depth to the helmsman every few seconds. At each Bedouin encampment along the bank the Arabs, big and small, male and female, would come out to shout greetings and run along the bank to watch us steaming by. On the *Mejidieh*, Captain Charley Cowley, who had been born in Baghdad and was regarded by the Turks as a Turkish national, exchanged news and banter with them to the unfailing amusement of the crew. You could always recognize his ship as he flew a pirate's skull and crossbones flag on his mast, having been proclaimed a pirate by the Turks. He paid the price for this later when captured by them. Other memories of unhurried journeys on the Tigris are of Arab fishermen skilfully casting their circular nets from the river's edge, or standing motionless in the water with poised trident spear, their wet naked bodies gleaming like bronze in the sun: and of the birds; the monotonous cry of the black partridge in the scrub; the sight of the speckled kingfisher hovering over water on quick-beating wings to dive like a stone, splash, rise, poise, and dive again and again.

In camp at Amara I had time to weed out a number of sepoys who were no longer fit for the severe fighting expected ahead.

35

Pyorrhoea in the older men and malarial spleens accounted for most of the rejects. Drafts of young recruits who had been sent out from India were put through intensive training and integrated into the companies. The regimental bombers practised throwing grenades without blowing themselves or others up and, in our spare time, we officers amused ourselves by trying to teach remount horses from the batteries the elements of polo! I went to hospital with a sharp attack of malaria, with high temperatures, rigors and delirium but soon recovered under the enormous doses of quinine prescribed at that time which made you severely deaf for days thereafter.

One night just after my return from hospital, while still feeling a bit giddy and deaf, I woke up with an uneasy feeling that someone was moving close by me in the palm leaf hut. Grabbing my revolver in the pitch darkness, I struck a match to light my hurricane lamp. I couldn't see anyone, nor did the sentry standing a few yards away, but in the morning I discovered that an Arab thief had stolen both my bivouac tent in its case and my warm serge uniform with other precious items. We were much pestered in all our camps by these sneak thieves who seemed to be able to slip in unobserved. Even when spotted the risk of firing at them at night was too great and their bodies so slippery with oil that they were able to escape capture.

Thieves! Ali Baba and the Forty Thieves! Baghdad! At about this time the name of this romantic city began to be mentioned in the camps with particular anticipation. After all we had advanced with very little difficulty more than halfway up the Tigris towards this almost legendary city. More significantly, the lure of such a city so temptingly placed up ahead, combined with the much-needed prestige which its capture would bestow on the Army throughout the East, proved irresistible to the High Command. As things stood, the obvious place to call a halt was at Amara, or, at the furthest, Kut-al-Amara, fifty miles further up the river, where the seasonably navigable Shatt-al-Hai channel left the Tigris to join the Euphrates which led to Nasiriyeh and the south. The country up to these points could probably have been held without too much difficulty but I have to say that the regiments of the 6th (Indian) Division would have been disappointed if it had been decided not to risk the gamble (which was to prove disastrous) of driving on towards Baghdad. We had the greatest confidence in ourselves and in our leader, General Townshend, and we anticipated making a triumphal entry into Baghdad, marching through the famous bazaars to general acclamation and hearing the muezzins calling the faithful to prayer from the four corners of the towering slender minarets. We could have hardly foreseen that the gamble would end in total failure and that our only entry would be as defiant prisoners of war six months later.

This dilemma was as old as warfare itself. In *Modern Egypt, Volume 2* p.75, Lord Cromer relates receiving the following advice from Lord Salisbury, the then Foreign Secretary:

> When you have permitted a military advance, the extent of that advance scarcely remains within your own discretion. It is always open to the military authorities to discover in the immediate vicinity of the area to which your orders confine them, some strategic position whose invaluable properties will repay ten times any risk or cost that its occupation may involve, and so, step by step, the imperious exactions of military necessity will lead you on into the desert.

And later, in 1890, in the same context, he wrote this strangely prophetic utterance:

> I would not be too much impressed by what the soldiers tell you about the strategic importance of these places. It is their way. If they were allowed full scope they would insist on the importance of garrisoning the Moon in order to protect it from Mars!

Chapter Six

Press on for Baghdad. Ctesiphon!

So the die was cast! The distant oracle had spoken and 'Onward for Baghdad' was the order of the day. But before such a move could take place we had first to capture the formidable Turkish defensive position astride the Tigris below the town of Kut-al-Amara (where we were to be besieged a few weeks later). This was a system of trenches and redoubts which later, greatly strengthened and made impassable by the river in flood, withstood all the desperate efforts made in 1916 by the forces sent to try to break the siege we were under and relieve us.

The 48th Pioneers, on this occasion, were in reserve but nevertheless were occupied in road making and digging emplacements to house the big bullock-drawn guns. My manuscript account of that September battle is punctuated with splurges and blots caused by the blast from each deafening discharge close behind us. From our position on the river bank we watched with sympathetic interest the near-miss splashes of Turkish shellfire aimed at the naval guns mounted individually on the small barges anchored in the river below us.

Before the start of the battle, I rode forward with the Brigade staff on a 'recce' and we unwittingly got a bit too close to the Turks, who loosed off a few shells at us for good measure. As well as their modern guns, the Turks had a number of ancient pieces and after one rather odd-sounding distant 'crump' the Staff Captain shouted to our elderly and rather deaf Brigadier General Fry, 'Mind that cannon ball General!' The General looked surprised and, looking around, murmured 'what cannon ball Gilchrist'? Luckily it bounced along past us, raising puffs of sand, but it would have made a nasty hole in one of us or one of our horses had we been in its path!

The main prong of our attack next day, a day of scorching sun, was successful in cutting in behind the main Turkish position but unfortunately the water in the marsh in that area, contrary to our information, proved brackish and undrinkable so that men, horses and mules had to cut short their encircling movement and make straight for the river. The result was that an important column of the Turkish army was able to make its escape to the north. We did, however, take 1,100 prisoners and occupied the town of Kut, situated in a loop of the river nearly halfway between Amara and Baghdad.

Riding in, I had a close look at the vacated enemy trenches. They were well-sited and protected by a deadly ditch filled with barbed wire, with machine-gun posts placed so as to be almost invisible from the front. A direct assault would certainly have resulted in the attackers suffering terrible casualties. I was amused to see a few of the ancient muzzle-loader guns with, alongside, piles of authentic cannon balls, in hidden emplacements trained across the river.

We remained at Kut throughout October and didn't think much of the place (we thought even less of it when we had to fall back on it in retreat a month later). A large Advanced Supply Depot was being built up and, in the intense heat and with the large number of horses and mules present, a vast plague of flies soon afflicted us, breeding at an incredible rate on the camp refuse. Going out for an early morning ride, we were not molested as the flies were still sluggish in the cold, but on returning our topis and shoulders were black with the brutes and our horses' heads were almost invisible because of the black cloud enveloping them. In our Mess tent we tried, with some success, to keep them down using Japanese clockwork fly traps and milk doped with formaldehyde, the latter being both deadly and messy!

Apart from the rather dubious joys of bathing in the river, there was good sport to be had in the evenings from shooting some of the vast numbers of sand grouse which flew in from the desert lying to our east to drink from the river. Shot guns and cartridges were available and marksmanship was naturally encouraged. Meanwhile, the regiment was engaged on a variety of pioneer works, including building jetties for the river steamers, while the main body of the Division had moved fifty-five miles north to Aziziyeh where we were well pleased to join them in early November 1915. At Aziziyeh all the talk was of the forthcoming assault onto the formidable Turkish defensive position at Ctesiphon, the fall of which would lay open the road to Baghdad.

Townshend's forces now consisted of the 6th (Indian) Division, reinforced by the 2nd Battalion, 7th Gurkha Rifles and two regiments of Punjabis. Townshend himself was, at that time, a remote figure to us at our level, almost unknown and rarely seen in the camps and trenches, unlike the popular and successful 'image conscious' generals of the Second World War. He nevertheless had a reputation as a brilliant if somewhat theatrical leader which appealed to us and we had good reason to have confidence in his military genius after the victorious campaign to date. It was not till near the end of the forthcoming disastrous siege that we began to have doubts and suspicions about his ability and to believe that, after all, this glittering figure had feet of clay!

A steady advance was made from Aziziyeh in mid-November 1915 and, after some minor scraps among tamarind and casuaria woods, the force concentrated on the river at Lajj. It was from here that, across the flat plain, we got our first view of the famous and historic old Arch of Ctesiphon, only twenty miles to the south of Baghdad.

This Arch, which dates from the sixth century, is the remains of the Palace of Chosroes, who was a famous Persian king and statesman. It is a segment of the great banqueting hall of which the ends and most of one side have fallen down. It rises to a height of almost 100 feet and forms an imposing feature in a flat landscape, visible for miles around. It is today a show site for tourists. There are other features of the Sassanian city that occupied this site near the river in the form of mounds, the most conspicuous being a high angular ridge known to us during the battle as High Wall.

A few days before the battle Lieutenant Venis told me, with a sad and comical smile, that owing to an inter-posting of officers in the battalion he would not be in the company led by Major Riddell, whom he greatly admired and with whom he had frequently been in action. However, on the very eve of the great day, I met him with a cheerful grin on his face and he told me that he had been transferred back to 'B' Company under Major Riddell.

The Turkish Army in front of us under Nur-ud-din had the strength of 18,000 regulars and an uncertain number of irregular formations of Arabs, mounted and on foot, equally dangerous to friend and foe! The Turks had fifty-two field guns. Our information as to their strength, defences and dispositions had been derived from spies, cavalry patrols and observations made by our two small aircraft. Unfortunately, one of the latter, flown by a Major Reilly, returning two days before the battle with the latest news and charts, had developed engine trouble and had been captured. Not only were we deprived of vital information of entirely new positions and reinforcements away out in the desert on the Turkish left flank but, worse still, the Turks captured details of recent seasonal changes in the course of the Tigris and its sandbanks from where our gunboats would be operating against them. Our naval strength had just been increased by the arrival of a new and competent river monitor, the *Firefly*, of shallow draught, good speed and firepower. Its brief and gallant career with us lasted a bare ten days before ending in disaster. The paddle yacht *Comet* and the old tug *Shaitan*, heroes of Amara, together with the tug *Sumara*, so valuable in Kut later, and a couple of horse barges, each with a 4.7-inch gun but without independent motive power, reinforced our artillery which had been recently increased by a battery of howitzers whose shells were capable of raising a heartening cloud of sand and vivid yellow smoke on landing. We had no mechanical transport at all, relying entirely on our tough mules pulling even tougher spring-less mule carts.

The battle commenced when we marched out of Lajj on the cold but clear night of 21 November in diverging columns. Our column was on the left and we followed the line of the telegraph

41

poles carrying telegraph wires all the way from Aleppo to Bushire on the Persian Gulf, but were now of course silent. We had three other columns operating on our right. The Turkish position extended from the river, with a short branch out on the right bank, out into the sand hills on the far left. There was an especially strong system of trenches and redoubts towards this flank, the key to the defence and labelled by General Townshend as VP or Vital Point. Nearer the centre was another strong redoubt (Water Redoubt), a mile or so to our column's right as we faced the Turkish trenches near the Arch. I have vivid and poignant memories of the Water Redoubt. The 48th Pioneers with the Ox and Bucks Light Infantry and the 119th Rajputana Indian Infantry were to attack the Turkish right which was supposed to be less strongly held.

We reached our designated position about midnight, apparently unobserved by the enemy, and quickly extended into battle formation, waiting in cold and discomfort for three hours in anxious anticipation of the dawn. It was a very dark night, no lights were allowed and, for direction, reliance was on compass bearing. I took up my position with my small squad beside the regimental reserve and near the mules which carried the reserves of ammunition, stretchers and medical panniers. Except in romantic novels, I don't think anyone goes into battle in cold blood singing the *Ode to Joy*. The medical knapsack over my shoulder lacked even a bottle of brandy, perhaps a wise omission!

We moved in for the attack, in extended order, at the first glimmerings of light, making rapidly for the Turkish trenches a mile or so ahead in the direction of the Arch of Ctesiphon. I accompanied the second line and the mules followed some distance behind. As the light strengthened we saw the whole plain on our right filled with our troops advancing steadily. The change from cold nervous waiting to active forward movement combined with this inspiring sight was very reassuring and, thus encouraged, the apprehensions of the night before rapidly faded.

So far Turkish reaction had been limited to a few shrapnel bursts over the leading troops, but soon the battle was joined in earnest over the whole front. The enemy trenches were clearly indicated by the massed puffs of our shrapnel shells bursting over them and the tremendous yellow flashes and thunderous explosions from our lyddite shells [ed. lyddite – a powerful explosive] as the howitzers opened up on the Vital Point (VP). We, on our part, began to come under increasing shell and long-range rifle fire from our left and front. I found it particularly disturbing to see little puffs of sand made by bullets hitting the ground close around and to hear the wicked whine of the ricochets whistling by with still enough force to disable you, if not worse, if they struck.

Meanwhile, far away on the right, our cavalry column had come under accurate fire and had lost so many horses that it failed to attain its objective, which was to pass behind the trenches of the Turkish extreme left flank and threaten the Turkish rear. The result was that they had to be content with dismounted action, with inconclusive results. It is probable that this failure largely accounted for our inability to gain the victory our efforts deserved, in spite of the greatest gallantry and heavy losses in the other sectors.

The assault on the 'VP' by Delamain's Brigade was carried through with the utmost dash and courage in the face of withering fire from the stubborn Turkish infantry, who were subjected to a full-scale artillery barrage from every gun we could bring to bear. The leading troops, the 2/7th Gurkhas and the 24th Punjabis suffered very heavy casualties. The Gurkhas, rushing in to attack and caught up in the barbed wire, slashed their way through with their kukris. Their Colonel, Lieutenant Colonel Powell, a huge man who towered above his little riflemen and was made even more conspicuous with his bright red face and white hair, is credited with completing the demor-alization of the defenders by the roaring fury of his language when he was inextricably hung up in the wire entanglement.

Meanwhile communications had become very much disor-ganized between the brigades on our right and our own brigade on the left flank. It appears that Townshend thought that he had overrun the Turkish trenches and redoubts in front of High Wall and the Arch, and he therefore deduced that the Water Redoubt could be pinched out between our brigade and the troops which had captured the 'VP'. He dispatched a scout at the gallop ordering our Brigadier to swing his attack to the right and to assault the Water Redoubt. Unfortunately at that moment we, with the Oxford and Buckinghamshire Light Infantry and others, were critically committed to a frontal attack on the still active system of trenches near the Arch. Hostile fire up to this point had not been heavy but was increasing in intensity every minute. I and my squad had to deal with a few light casualties, using the field dressings carried by each man, supplemented by additional material from my surgical knapsack. I detached one orderly to remain in charge of those wounded unable to come further forward, with the necessarily vague orders as to their disposal: there was a field ambulance following up some distance back, but it was not expected to set up a casualty receiving station until the course of the battle became clearer.

It is a great tribute to our troops and their officers that the extremely difficult manoeuvre of changing the direction of attack to half-right in mid-assault was performed with speed. Nevertheless, it inevitably resulted in some confusion and the intermingling of units, carried out as it was under increasingly heavy Turkish fire. My regiment was heavily enfiladed as we crossed for nearly a mile in front of the Turkish trenches at a distance of only a few hundred yards. We then came up against the still intact Water Redoubt.

At this moment I felt a terrific thump on the left side of my head which knocked me over, piercing my topi and sending it flying. The world was going around in circles and, when I put my hand to my left ear and found it covered in blood, I concluded that I had had it! In point of fact a bullet had gone through my ear and banged against the mastoid bone where one's balancing apparatus is located. Fortunately the horizon soon steadied up and, after being attended to and bandaged by my 'doctor babu', after a short rest I felt able to continue and catch up with the battle.

In the meantime, the formidable Water Redoubt and the trenches around it had fallen to a final bayonet charge. Our Colonel, no longer dyspeptic, and the Adjutant Burdett, who were the only officers of ours left unwounded, supported by a handful of sepoys, had rushed a trench full of Turks. Then there had followed a period of uncertainty between the two sides as to who had surrendered to whom but the question was soon settled by the arrival of more and more sepoys. Large numbers of Turks were quickly disarmed and herded to the rear.

I can never forget the heartrending scene in front of that Redoubt. The desert around was dotted thick with fallen figures, some motionless in unnatural attitudes, others rolling about in agony and distress, a few walking, hobbling or staggering about. A particularly horrifying sight was one of our Sikh sepoys sitting on the ground and beckoning to me to come over. The whole of his lower jaw had been shot clean away and the stump of his ragged tongue was hanging out. He indicated he wanted a sip of water but he was not able to swallow.

Near him , among the dead and wounded Jats of his company, lay a quiet temporary officer of our regiment, not at all an heroic type, with a drawn sword in his hand, clutched in death. It was most unusual for an officer to take a sword into battle and having done that he had then made the surprising gesture of drawing it to give himself courage at a moment when any heart might fail. His company commander had already been killed earlier in the action.

Not far off, and within a few yards of the Turkish barbed wire, I was attracted by a feeble cry to poor little Lieutenant Venis, shot through the body, paralysed and dying. I hurried to his side but when I got to him all he did, in spite of his own agony and distress, was to point to a figure lying face-downwards just ahead of him and cry in a broken voice, 'Oh! Spackie, they've killed Riddell'. And there was our splendid Riddell, shot through the head and body, his fair hair clotted with blood and sand. I gave the poor boy a strong shot of morphine and he died a few minutes later with his head on my knee.

Venis had come to us just after the Shaiba battle with three other officers of the Indian Army Reserve. He was very small and looked like a jockey. In fact, he had been a keen amateur rider in Burma and he had a jaunty, almost cheeky, manner not entirely approved of by the Colonel. His father was a planter in

45

the Mergui Archipelago in southern Burma. He liked to give the impression that he was irresistible to the opposite sex and his conversation was often interspersed with comments and gestures tending to support this idea. His Burmese bearer, one Maung Shwee, was rather hot-tempered and liable, if annoyed, to produce a kriss and make threatening gestures. This excessive loyalty to his master's interests sometimes got Maung Shwee into arguments but he was cautiously respected by the Mess staff.

I still had most of my squad of stretcher bearers with me and, as we were near the Water Redoubt, I began to collect the wounded into that area at about noon. It at least afforded us a source of water supply, pretty stagnant and needing the removal of some dead bodies before it could be used. I was the only RMO of our column still able to function so I had many casualties from other units to deal with apart from our own. By mid-afternoon I had at least 200 casualties lying about the Redoubt in groups, with some able to give a little help to their fellows, but I was becoming quite exhausted in trying to minister to their wounds and in organizing the operation. The battle was more or less over for the time being, although a strong counterattack by the Turks was being held off around the V P away to our right, where brisk firing could be heard.

At this moment, to my infinite relief, Padre Spooner (brother of the famous Lancashire cricketer) rode up on a mule. He was attached to Colonel Donegan's field ambulance and had been sent forward to find a suitable place for the field ambulance to be set up. After a few words with me, he dug his heels into his mule and set off at the gallop to bring it up. When the ambulance mules and carts arrived I very thankfully handed over my patients to the staff.

I mentioned earlier how at Shaiba my nerves were steadied by borrowing a rifle and taking a pot-shot or two at the advancing Turks, after meticulously removing my Red Cross brassard! At Ctesiphon, my head stretcher bearer turned up at the Water Redoubt looking thoroughly ashamed and carrying a rifle.

'Havildar Dayal Singh,' I said, 'where have you been?'

'Sahib', he replied, 'my friend Mohan Singh was killed and you were wounded; it was no good being a stretcher-bearer so I got a rifle and went forward.'

I found that he had joined the handful of sepoys who were with the Colonel and consequently he was one of the first into the Turkish trenches. He was given an award for gallantry and promoted but this incident was hardly a good example to other stretcher bearers! It seemed to me, but I was too junior and diffident to say so at the time, that the policy of sending RMOs into battle in the open desert accompanying the second line of the attack was a foolish concept. We were expensively trained and very difficult to replace yet we incurred almost as great a risk of being killed or wounded as the combatants, especially as it was well known that fire directed at the leading attackers was usually aimed too high so that we who followed got the overs. In battle we were only able to put on a field dressing, give a shot of morphine and make a collecting point for casualties. In later years each soldier was trained to do this 'first aid'. It was argued that our presence with the troops gave them confidence but quite often a unit went into battle with an MO who had only just joined it. In my case, I had been with the regiment since before we left India and up to the present my luck had been in, and indeed it continued, but several of my colleagues with other units had not been so lucky. Indeed some had been killed.

Soon after Colonel Donegan's field ambulance had started working, I began helping them, but I was very exhausted and in shock and when they gave me a cup of tea I brought it straight up again. Donegan, like a good Irishman, knew the remedy. He produced from one of his panniers a small bottle of champagne and poured me out a glass, naturally for the sake of good company taking a glass himself! Never have I had a more marvellous drink. Almost, one might say, it saved my life, for soon after I was able to drink a bowl of soup and to follow it with a dish of stew (Irish, of course), falling fast asleep in spite of the battle flaring up afresh as the Turkish counterattack was beaten off. Intermittent fighting continued through most of the night; a matter of some concern, for we could have easily been overrun as there was a gap in our hastily organized defence line.

When, rested and restored, I rejoined my regiment at dawn next day, the 23 November, the picture was far from reassuring. We had lost 60 per cent of our regimental strength in dead and wounded. Of our ten British officers, four had been killed and four wounded and all the twelve Indian officers except one had become casualties. Of the whole fighting force engaged, numbering about 10,000, the casualty list was later given officially as 4,593. Behind us we had almost no reserves whilst our reinforcements were only just reaching Basra nearly 500 miles away down river. In addition to our burden of casualties, having 1,300 Turkish prisoners on our hands embarrassed us. These were evacuated to India; God knows how! Houghton's Brigade, of which we were part, had suffered frightful losses. A Company Sergeant Major of the Ox and Bucks Light Infantry was his acting Brigade Major. I remember seeing Colonel Lethbridge of that historic regiment (the 43rd) walking up and down at his regimental concentration post looking a picture of utter woe, having lost so many fine officers and gallant men in the battle. I had known them well in cantonments in India just before the war. Their MO was one of the casualties.

Although the main Turkish position was in our hands, the village near the 'Arch' and an area near the river were held by actively hostile and menacing troops, freshly arrived by steamer from Baghdad. A tactically important mound, 'Gurkha Mound', was attacked and captured by the 2/7th Gurkhas, providing some relief to the situation, though how those Gurkhas with their short legs got across from the 'VP' far on the right to 'Gurkha Mound' on the extreme left almost passes comprehension.

'My little men can fight' protested their Colonel, 'but don't expect them to march great distances on the flat as well!'

Fortunately our naval guns on the river were near at hand and provided support in great style when a target presented itself.

I had little to do after evacuating all our own casualties, the policy being to retain only fit men within the unit. I was therefore detailed to go over to 'VP' and help evacuate the wounded, collected by a field ambulance there. I was not clear as to the exact direction to take but started out early next day by

48

following the irregular line of Turkish trenches. These were in such a mess, filled with water, mud, barbed wire and half-buried bodies that I soon preferred to risk it in the open. On this flank the Turks were making intermittent counterattacks and our position was by no means secure; a situation complicated by a shortage of ammunition, so many of the mules which carried the ammunition having been killed or gone astray. However, at this time there was only occasional sniping from the watchful enemy. I got a bit lost wandering about trying to find the field ambulance but luckily was hailed by one of their officers who sternly told me to get down in the trench and stop attracting fire! I hastily obeyed and we all set to work, protected by a slight ridge, loading up a convoy of mule carts and sending them off across on a rough track in small batches. As soon as they were in the open, they came under shell fire, there being nothing to distinguish them as an ambulance convoy, and as a result some of the mules bolted, fortunately in the right direction, but causing agony for the wounded, all crowded together in the spring-less carts.

The sight of many such frightful battle wounds was much more shocking when seen on the battlefield away from the ordered and professional atmosphere of the operating theatre where one had seen them before. When the poor wretches reached the river that evening, they were loaded as close together as possible on the open decks of iron barges to save room. Many never reached the field hospitals, much less the base hospitals, nor even got a change of dressing until they arrived at Basra a week later. The conditions on the slow moving barges were indescribable. Many of the injured suffered from acute dysentery for which those in charge had no treatment facilities. Later there was a great public scandal about it, but I do not think, from personal experience, that the blame could be placed fairly on the medical staff in the field units, who were grossly overworked in the most difficult conditions imaginable in active warfare. In those days there were no helicopters or even any mechanical transport to provide lift, only the humble mule cart and river transport!

On 25 November there was an ominous lull in the fighting. This caused an atmosphere of uncertainty, almost amounting to dismay, among the regiments as to what the next move would be. As a precaution, our weakened forces were withdrawn to a defensive position centred on 'High Wall' and that evening I climbed up the steep side of it to the flat wide top where there was an observation post overlooking the battlefield. The 'Arch' and its adjoining village of Sulman Pak were quite close to our left. In the far distance to the north was a line of low sand hills towards the Diyala river where it joins the Tigris and it was in this direction that observation was intently focused.

Sure enough, after a while, a cloud of dust could be made out in the far distance and not long after this a column of marching troops could be seen clearly, winding its way through the sand hills. These could only be Turks, and if they continued on the same heading it was evident that they would outflank us and reach the river below us, seriously threatening our river transport on which we were entirely dependent. All our supplies and ammunition came by river and all our sick and wounded were evacuated down it on the return journeys. Even the gunboats were threatened. We were not surprised therefore when orders were issued for us to abandon our hard won positions and march immediately back to Lajj.

You can imagine how we felt. There was a sense of bitter frustration, despondency even, barren toil endured in vain and bitter loss as we retreated wearily back across the plain that night, back to Lajj from which we had set out so confidently only four days earlier to fight the desperate battle at Ctesiphon.

Chapter Seven

Retreat to Kut

When, next morning at 0200 hrs, we marched (trudged would be more accurate) back to Lajj, weary and apprehensive, we were further depressed when we arrived by having to arouse and then grimly sober up the Reservist Officer in charge of the small depot established there. Having got ourselves a peg of whisky and a couple of dry biscuits, we dossed down in our area of the defence perimeter, half expecting to be attacked at dawn by the oncoming Turks. As I settled down gratefully in my sleeping bag on the bare ground, I felt a pang of pity for the tired men posted as sentries on immediate alert duties.

As it turned out we had a day's reprieve as the Turks had halted on the recent battlefield. This gave us time to take breath and counsel before continuing our retreat, a day's march down the river to Aziziyeh where we expected to fall back on a much larger advanced base. At Lajj we left some tents standing and the fires burning with, alongside, a few unfit mules tethered so as to make the enemy a bit more cautious in their advance. No mines were laid – our Sappers had not got any out there!

A combination of skill of a high order, plus some luck, brought the vast and varied fleet of steamers, tugs, launches, barges, pontoons and minor craft down the precarious reaches of the fast flowing river. This must have been a nightmare trip for those marvellous naval types, who never failed us. However that was a pleasure cruise compared with what was in store for them when the Turks caught up with us two days later.

There was no satisfactory defensive position at Aziziyeh, nor anywhere above Kut. At Kut, in its loop of the river, we had a very large supply depot for the whole division and ample space. By retiring to Kut we would command the Hai branch of the Tigris River leading towards the Euphrates, shorten our tenuous line of communication and facilitate our chances of reinforcement or relief.

The only incident I recall during our short stop at Aziziyeh was an outbreak of looting at the depot when clothing and equipment was stolen by a few Indian troops, chiefly by miscellaneous followers, indicating a lowering of morale. It was easily suppressed by small squads of troops from regiments whose discipline under their officers remained unimpaired. The paradox was that only the next day great quantities of these stores were deliberately destroyed by fire to avoid them falling into the hands of the enemy. To have argued that a policy of 'take what you need and can carry on the march' would have been sensible, even if properly controlled, would not have been very safe or practicable and would have flown against all Service tradition.

Meanwhile, it was known that the enemy were following us up, albeit cautiously, so after leaving Aziziyeh on 30 November we made a relatively short march and halted well before dusk at a sharp bend in the river at a place called Um al Tabul. During this march we were much heartened by the splendid sight of a regiment of British Cavalry, the 14th Hussars, riding north to join our Cavalry Brigade.

The reason that the march was short was that it was necessary to coordinate the withdrawal of the ships on the river with that of the troops on land, each being dependent on each other. At this point the serpentine windings of the River Tigris were even more preposterous than usual. At the bend where we camped, only half a mile from our withdrawal route, we were able to offer some protection to the shipping crowded under the high banks of the river.

At this camp the troops were for once allowed to cook a hot meal and, although no lights were permitted after dark, the dying embers of the fires may have been visible from a considerable distance. We were nevertheless surprised, as we prepared for sleep, when a few shells fell on the camp from the direction from which the Turks were expected and it alerted us that a force including artillery was closing in on us.

My own duties on the march and in camp were twofold. On this occasion, after dealing with the few sores and sicknesses amongst the sepoys, I organized an ad hoc evening meal for our officers, all sitting on the ground or on panniers. Our old Mess cook was none too well and he had to be jollied along. He repaid my attention on this and other occasions by producing, under the greatest difficulties, some sort of a meal that most of us were able to eat with good appetite and digestion.

In view of the alarm caused by the impact of the shells, all the carts were kept fully loaded ready for an immediate move off at first light, and our guns were deployed ready to pound any target that might threaten us. A messenger was sent off at the gallop to recall Melliss's Brigade which had already marched off south. The messenger found the Brigade in the middle of the night and they did an abrupt about-turn and were able to take a significant part in the action next day.

As dawn broke on 1 December an amazing sight greeted our unbelieving eyes. At a range of no more than 3,000 yards we beheld a very large and well-organized camp set out in long lines of white tents, with horses and mules being groomed or led off in strings to the river; in fact a busy but unsuspecting camp about to start its morning chores and getting ready for a leisurely start to the day after a forced march. A Gunner's dream! Our Gunners didn't wait to rub their eyes but prepared to take immediate advantage of this unexpected opportunity. Daylight comes quickly in the desert. No sooner was the tantalizing target visible, and its range registered, than every gun in our field batteries and those in our ships nearby roared into action. Before the scene was blotted out by the dust and smoke from our shrapnel and shells as they burst upon it like rain, we just had time to see the confusion caused in that camp, horses careering about, tents crashing down and men running around in all directions. The covering force of our infantry was able to add to the confusion by long-range rifle fire.

We learned later that this pursuing Turkish Army comprised four divisions of which the troops of one were completely demoralized by the sudden and unexpected barrage of shells that descended upon them in their exposed position in the open plain. Their General was killed and the troops fled in disorder. Unfortunately for us, another more experienced division was positioned to a flank with artillery able to enfilade our ships deep in the angle of the river with disastrous results.

While all this was going on, my regiment, the 48th Pioneers, was detailed to get our big divisional transport column away from the scene and escort it safely south to Kut as fast as we could go, while another detachment acted as rearguard. On account of several deep wadis, we had to take the carts a full half-mile towards the Turkish lines before we could swing right-handed on to the regular track to the south. This was an unhealthy manoeuvre during which we were sniped at irregularly and progress was not helped by the tendency of some 'drabis' to cut off instinctively to the right with their carts before clearing the wadis. This tendency was increased when one of the drabis toppled off the top of his heavily laden AT cart. I forget if he was wounded or merely frightened but I do remember that a syce nearby, riding one of our chargers, was knocked out of the saddle with a severe bullet wound. I felt it was safer to march to leeward of one of the large carts.

Even when we had marched beyond the range of the action we had our own anxieties as, not only did we have the responsibilities of escorting the 1,300 Turkish prisoners captured at Ctesiphon, but we had been warned that the powerful and predatory Sheik Ghadban with 5,000 horsemen was hovering on our desert flank. We could not understand why he did not fall upon the long and valuable column of transport which we were guarding inadequately. Judging by what happened to some unfortunates who subsequently fell into the hands of nomadic Arabs in isolated desert encounters, the more prepossessing of us might have suffered 'a fate worse than death' or equally painful mutilation had such an encounter gone against us.

We marched all that day almost without a halt and, late in the evening, crossed a bridge over a steep wadi at a place we named

'Monkey Village', camping safely but very exhausted on the far side. Many of us officers marched on foot with the men, putting sick men on our chargers. Most of the drabis, well swathed in blankets, travelled asleep on top of their loads, trusting to the mules to follow in the tracks of the cart in front, just as in India one sees the patient bullock carts lumbering steadily along, mile after dusty mile, with their human cargo stretched out fast asleep on top of a pile of household cargo.

As darkness drew on, I was guiding my medical cart and our Mess cart as best I could when I noticed that, at a bend in the track ahead, each cart was swinging out a foot more than the previous cart towards a steep bank. I just succeeded in straightening up my two carts, the last of my battalion's, by pushing and tugging the bridle of the nearest mule. However, when I dashed back shouting about the danger to the carts following close behind, I found the drabis were asleep and in spite of my efforts to drag at the mules, the outer wheel of the next cart went over the edge and I had to jump clear to avoid the top-heavy cart as it heeled over. Inevitably the next cart followed, crashing down the bank on top of it. Two more followed before the sounds of disaster and distress roused those in charge to the danger. I did not wait to help sort out the chaos.

We reached Kut, which we had left with such high hopes four weeks earlier, soon after noon on 2 December after marching fifty miles in thirty hours. At once we began cooking food and sending it back to those troops who had the task of holding off the enemy with the aim of gaining time for the river transport to get away from the dangerous trap at Um al Tabul. At the same time we started digging a big series of trenches and gun emplacements in preparation for the anticipated siege.

We must now go back briefly in time to follow what happened to the river flotilla after we had moved back with the rear echelon to Kut.

The reason we stopped at Um al Tabul for the night on our withdrawal from Aziziyeh to Kut was that the river flotilla was not expected to get past that point owing to the devious course taken by the river and because of its shallowness. It was at its annual lowest level and was difficult to navigate because it had an unpredictable pattern of sandbanks which alternated with deep water channels in which the water ran fast in some places whilst it eddied sluggishly in others. In addition, high and gusty winds made keeping under control the steamers and tugs a very difficult task, as they had unwieldy and heavily laden barges attached, whilst they steamed at speed down stream. Those in charge of the naval vessels had a nightmare task supervising the convoy, in view of the great diversity of craft involved, which ranged from big river steamers down to launches trailing strings of bellums, danaks and the pontoons of the bridging train.

The heroic old *Shaitan* was the first to go. She had her day of glory at the capture of Amara and had since worn out her aged machinery and strained her ancient plates in gallant support of us at Ctesiphon. At Um al Tabul she ran aground once too often and then came under close fire from the enemy. Some of her overstrained plates parted, she sprang an uncontrollable leak and subsided with her lower deck awash. Her sister ships made superhuman attempts to get her clear, but, with Arabs and Turks only yards away, she was abandoned after her crew and any useful equipment had been taken off onto other ships. More disasters were to follow.

The river level was so low that it was difficult to spot most of the ships from the land but unfortunately the brand new *Firefly*, pride of the fleet on the river, had a superstructure and mast so tall as to be visible far off, especially to the gunnery observers of the Turkish division established on the right bank of the river overlooking the fatal bend. She was not only a conspicuous target for the enemy guns but also gave the enemy a good indication of where the other vessels were, both big and small. An unlucky direct hit on the *Firefly*'s engine room caused a spectacular explosion. A fireman member of the engine crew was severely scalded, others were wounded and the ship was immobilized. The *Comet* came up to rescue her but, in attempting to take her in tow, was hit and set on fire. The *Sumara*, an armed tug, now made a successful attempt to take off the crews of both ships, though failing to take off the fatally injured fireman and one or two others. The breach-blocks of their guns were thrown into the river but the *Firefly* was not blown up because of the injured ratings on board. The *Sumara* just got clear before the Turks reached the riverbank alongside her.

During all this time the rest of the shipping, with its huge barges full of ammunition, food supplies and wounded was struggling to get away down river without getting in each others' way. Accounts given of subsequent happenings are, not surprisingly, confused. I was told a number of different accounts but all agreed that, under the desperate and urgent circumstances prevailing at the time, every possible effort was made, especially by the Royal Navy vessels, to save personnel and material. Sadly, one barge carrying wounded, miscellaneous detachments and stores became hopelessly stranded and had to be abandoned with Arabs already swarming up her sides. There was a story of one portly and sedentary Colonel of the Supply Department plunging through mud and water to gain the bank, climbing out and then making a brisk sprint across country to join our retreating column; but for the rest, it is a sad tale of great material loss and of shameless looting and abuse by the Bedouin Arabs before the Turkish regulars arrived to take control. The unfortunate prisoners taken from the barges, most of them sick or wounded, were taken off to Baghdad and thence to the newly constructed prisoner of war camps in Anatolia, 1,200 miles away across the Toros Mountains, where unimaginably to us at the time, we too were to join them some months later.

A majority of the river steamers carrying wounded from Ctesiphon had already gone down river making for Basra. Of those involved at the Um al Tabul bend all ultimately fetched up at Kut, with the exceptions I have named, although they had to defend themselves all the way down the river from nomadic Arabs, who closed in, as was their wont, to harass those in adversity and woe betide any of our lads who fell into their merciless hands.

Chapter Eight

Besieged in Kut

When, on 2 December 1915, we marched wearily back with the Divisional Transport Column into Kut it was with the knowledge that we were almost certainly going to be besieged but we were also confident that we should soon be relieved by forces coming up the river from Basra. The Turks, after the severe handling we had given them at Um al Tabul, were only following us up cautiously so that we had a short interval to get sorted out and prepared.

During all the fighting and marching we had done in the past month, we had been living on field scale rations. My responsibilities as officer running the Mess prompted me now to take such steps as were possible to secure a good additional food supply. As soon as I had dealt with a rather heavy morning sick parade, I took three mules equipped with their panniers into the town, which lay about a mile behind our lines, and bought up a lot of tinned food from an Arab shop. This was an inspired action as later in the day on 3 December, all local supplies of every description were commandeered by the Director of Supplies! I also got hold of several cases of provisions and drinks, already the property of our Mess, which we had parked in our Brigade's supply depot when we advanced north. So I returned in triumph late in the afternoon to our lines! Among the more questionable items was a case of tinned butter from the Aligarh Dairy in India which had been with us throughout the previous summer and had, in consequence, attained such a degree of rancidity that it was voted totally inedible by even the least fastidious. However, months later, towards the end of the siege, I cautiously produced a tin of it, revolting in appearance and smelling and tasting like sump oil, and it was accepted, if not gratefully, at least without protest! It represented 'fat' in a diet that contained absolutely none.

A few days later I secured another welcome prize, a barrel of beer, obtained for free from the Supply and Transport Corps because their main supply park was so placed as to be very vulnerable to the Turkish shellfire which had begun to pour in at this time. Two or three barrels had been holed by shrapnel and so the rest was distributed on demand to any unit which applied promptly; first come, first served. As I had my ear close to the ground in such matters, I was well up in the queue and soon had our barrel settled in an excavation in the wall of our Mess dugout. Its contents lasted a surprisingly long time, with no complaints of it 'going off'.

There has been much argument as to the correctness of the command decision to stand at Kut and await relief. In those days it was customary to accept without question orders from above. Junior officers were less critical of their superiors, at least openly, than is the habit today, the advice given being 'keep your mouth shut and your bowels open'! In spite of the disastrous events of the preceding fortnight, which might have raised doubts in our minds, we still (for a little longer) had boundless confidence in Major General Townshend, if not in Lieutenant General Nixon, the Corps Commander. The latter had preceded us down from the battlefield with his gilded staff on the *Malamir*, known to us as the 'Gin Palace', to Basra in order to organize our relief. However it was said that he had refused to delay his departure despite the fact that acceptance of a short delay would have allowed a barge loaded with wounded to have been attached to his steamer.

We had such confidence in Townshend's military intuitions that, not realizing the difficulties facing the Relieving Force, every time, during the coming months, we heard of its fresh failure to break through, under a succession of generals, we in the trenches of Kut were wont to complain:

'Why don't they send an aeroplane to pick up Townshend and put him in command of the relief? He would soon get through!'

Looking back, it is clear that at least one fatal error was made at an early stage by our leaders in Kut. No accurate or even approximate estimate was made of the total food supply available in Kut, nor of how long could it be made to last, nor of how much longer it could be made to spin out if we forced the Arab population to leave. Presumably the latter drastic step was deemed morally unjustifiable and politically unacceptable, although militarily it made sense. It became even more unacceptable later in the siege as the Turks simply shot down those civilians trying to get away across the river on rafts and inflated skins from the beleaguered town. Our strength, in round figures, was British Officers 300, British Other Ranks 2,850, Indian Officers and Sepoys 8,250, Army followers 3,500 and some 6,000 local Arabs, totalling approximately 21,000. The defended area within the deep loop of the River Tigris was about a mile across and two miles deep. At the downstream corner we had made a fort with a strong system of redoubts and traverses connected right across to the river bank upstream by three lines of trenches, one front-line with two supporting trenches. My regiment was located just behind the second supporting trench line, much too near a field battery for comfort as it attracted the attention of the Turkish gunners! As compensation, our Pioneers, being specialists in defensive works, made for us secure and comfortable dugouts roofed with galvanized iron covered with a layer of earth. Each officer had his own dugout in which he scratched little niches in the mud walls for his small possessions. All very snug and tidy until the floods poured in. This happened when the heavy rains came in January!

Across the river at the upstream corner a strong contingent held a small village in order to guard the entrance to the Hai channel which required periodical re-supply by night by the *Sumara*, our sole remaining armed ship. At the downstream corner, by the fort, the Sapper Sandes constructed a bridge of boats with the few danaks he had saved, eked out with some Arab dhows. The width of the river varied from 300 to 450 yards.

The Turks arrived in force on the 5 December and immediately encircled us, cutting us off from downstream. However, before that event Townshend had sent the cavalry and most of the mule corps south over the boat-bridge to join the Relieving Force. The far end of this boat-bridge was guarded rather lightly by Indian troops. On 9 December the Turks made a strong attack on this bridgehead and, after a determined resistance, it was overrun, with many casualties including the officer in command who was killed. The same day the enemy bombarded the town, the fort and the frontline, following up by formally calling for our surrender. A very rude reply was returned.

The overrunning of the bridge of boats was too serious a situation to accept but we obviously did not want to lose valuable bridging material by blowing up the bridge from our end. It was decided to blow the bridge from the other end while also cutting the anchor ropes which stabilized the bridge in the middle, a difficult and dangerous operation while the bank at the far end was held by the Turks. Two officers volunteered for this job, a Sapper friend of ours, Matthews, and a Gurkha officer, Sweet. They were allocated a small party of Indian Sappers and some of our 48th Pioneers, the party to be given covering fire by Gurkha riflemen. The plan was for the party to creep unseen across the bridge at night, fix explosives in at least two places, cut the retaining cables, light the fuses and then scuttle back before being either wiped out by the Turks or blown up with the bridge. Nowadays such a desperate enterprise might not be attempted for so small a tactical gain. Maybe it would be a suitable task for men trained as frogmen but no such equipment had at that time been invented.

Matthews, cheerful as ever, dined in our Mess that night and in spite of having had many hours to plan the operation and therefore appreciate its extreme danger, he seemed outwardly calm. There is a saying that all Sappers are mad, married and Methodist! As we shook him by the hand and wished him good luck, it was not easy to conceal our apprehension and the fear that we might not see him again.

It was a very dark night and we waited with great anxiety for what seemed an eternity. Finally we heard two great thumping explosions and we knew that they had done it. Carrying dynamite charges, they had crossed to the furthest pontoon, fixed them to the woodwork under the roadway, set the fuses and hurried silently back, cutting the tethering cables most methodically as they moved. As they reached our shore the bridge blew up. Only one man was wounded. The medals awarded to the leaders of the operation were well deserved.

When the Turks first arrived opposite us our defences were far from ready and they seized the opportunity of making an immediate attack. It was easily beaten off and pressure was relieved when a large body of them marched south past the fort to prepare a position from which to oppose the Relieving Force, which was being disembarked at Basra to be sent up river in driblets. Within a few days, however, strong forces of Turks made resolute and repeated attacks on our frontline from their trenches and from the saps dug close up within yards of ours. Much ammunition had to be expended in repelling them and orders were soon given not to fire unless a target was clearly identified:

24 December. From my diary. Last day or two have been comparatively peaceful though it is quite unsafe to leave the trench system by day or night. Shell fire has now dropped from 2,000 a day to a mere 50 in the whole defended area. The Turks are only about sixty to eighty yards away in some places.

We have sent our shaving mirrors up to the frontline to make periscopes.--- Rumour names 28 Dec for our relief.--- We still can get fresh milk and eggs (now three pence each) at night from the town.---There is a cat which lives comfortably in a chink in the Mess wall among the sand-bags beside the beer barrel.---We keep up our spirits and talk of starting an Alarm and Despondency Box with a fine of one rupee for every pessimistic remark.

In fact, we younger officers at this stage of the siege were able to treat most things as subjects for jokes and horseplay, especially when friends from other units visited.

My medical duties with the regiment were trivial, being chiefly concerned with minor fevers and digestive upsets, the policy being to retain in lines only day-to-day sick, more serious cases being sent to hospital in the town a mile away. As for my responsibilities for running the Mess, there was no scope for enterprise and I left most of that to the cook and Mess Havildar.

Needing something more useful to do, I arranged to go into the town three mornings a week to help the doctors in the General Hospital by treating those wounded by shell or small-arms fire. There was also an increasing incidence of dysentery and serious fevers and chest complaints. These included TB, together with an occasional case of appendicitis or other surgical emergency which provided me with a little more professional interest. We had no nurses, only RAMC and nursing orderlies, many of whom could help only in the most elementary way.

In mid-December the Turkish attack became much more determined, especially in the direction of the fort, which remained their main objective. We were subjected to frequent and heavy bombardment and to the sapping moving ever closer to our wire which made the life of sentries an anxious one. This cat and mouse 'game', also much employed on the Western Front, where the enemy tried to mine under our wire while our Pioneers undertook countermining, with the associated task of establishing listening posts, was carried on unceasingly. A local sortie revealed an extensive system of enemy earthworks going right up to the fort and resulted in a number of Turks being killed right there. I went up to the firing line with one of our officers to view through a periscope the enemy's trenches and barbed wire and saw earth being thrown up from one of their saps barely fifty yards away.

Finally, on Christmas Eve, the Turks brought up some of their best troops and, after an intense barrage, launched a furious attack on our battered positions and trenches at the fort. After desperate hand-to-hand combat, with crippling losses to both sides, the enemy was thrown out but not before a Volunteer Eurasian Battery had fought gallantly at point-blank range, using shells, bombs and anything they could lay their hands on

63

in their efforts to assist the sorely pressed sepoys, many of whom were lying dead or wounded under and against the crumbled ramparts and traverses.

Little deterred, the Turks renewed their attack, with even more violence, in the darkness early on Christmas morning. The battle raged, swaying back and forth with unrelenting fury, noise, dust, blood and shouting until a very confused situation developed where the Turks had gained one section of the fort and from it threatened not only the rest of the fort but also the whole of the frontline beyond it. One company of the 48th Pioneers had been based in the fort for some days, patching up the breaches made by Turkish guns and renewing the wire (a particularly dangerous task). Now, in the darkness, they were called upon to retake the vital sector which had been overrun by a detachment of Turks, who were equipped with bombs and hand grenades which they lobbed over each traverse while remaining under cover from our rifle fire. Our sepoys suffered many casualties but materially helped in throwing out the enemy and saving the critical situation. The defence of the fort that night was rendered more difficult for our troops who were called out in the emergency because they were unfamiliar with the complicated trench system and because of the confusion caused by not knowing which portions of the defences were still in our hands and which were occupied by the Turks. The fighting all took place in the darkness of a winter's night, in clouds of dust and acrid smoke, amidst a continuous din of bombs exploding, the crack of firearms and shouting in several languages. Hell could not be much worse!

Sunrise revealed hundreds of dead Turks in the ruins of the fort and even more dead and wounded in front of it. We managed to bring in a few of the wounded who lay close at hand and some others managed to crawl one way or the other. Having failed to get any cooperation from the local Turkish commander, there was no option but to leave the dead and some mortally wounded men caught up in the tangle of barbed wire to their fate, moaning pitifully until they died of their wounds or for lack of water in the blazing sun, hours, or even days later.

The gruesome corpses were a very noticeable reminder of the battle, both by day and night.

Our losses in desperate defence of the fort were over 300. The Turks lost 1,000 killed. This Christmas Day attack was significant as it was the last attempt by the enemy to capture Kut by direct assault. The diary again:

Christmas Day 1915. All is peace now after the great attack on the fort in the night. We lost four of our sepoys killed and had twenty-one wounded, including Neumann, making our regimental casualties since 21 November a total of 350, of which 100 are dead.---I was able to go to a short Christmas service in the serai with the Adjutant.---They say that the Relieving Force cannot get here for another fortnight.

31 December. Fairly quiet this last week. The Relieving Force is to start from Ali Gharbi any day and should be here by 8 Jan as it is said that the Turks will not try to stop them(!!). We are on a three-quarter scale of rations and as I have a lot of tinned stores for the Mess we do quite well. Laundry is a big problem.

The Turkish guns now turned their attention to the town, which came under daily pounding, causing much damage but few casualties. They also spared a few shells for our batteries behind the frontline near us, causing more annoyance than damage, except when one chance shell fell on a dugout full of gunners, killing several. Another hit the all-important *Sumara* (Tudway, RN), damaging its steering gear. She was the only remaining means of carrying supplies to the detachment on the other side of the river near the Hai canal. Somehow the Sappers improvised the essential spare parts to repair the damage, relieving us of what would have been the very difficult task of withdrawing this important post.

As well as the damage done to the town by shell fire, which caused more alarm than casualties, further destruction was done by us. When firewood became short, and when unexposed passageways between buildings were required, holes were knocked right through Arab houses, resulting in a deal of protest and consternation, not to mention scandalizing the stricter Moslems by the invasion of their harems. To compensate them, we built passages sheltered by matting screens down to the river bank so that the women could draw water without being fired on by snipers from the opposite bank; an annoying activity at this time.

A touch of comedy was lent to the bombardment of the town by a very ancient and prestigious mortar, duplicate I suspect of the famous one used by Emperor Theodore of Abyssinia against Napier in 1868. We had actually captured this monumental piece of ordnance at Ctesiphon, and for a short time held it, so I knew something about it. Made of brass, with much embellishment and ornamentation, it threw in a high arc a great round shell weighing 200 pounds. To the Turks its prestige and sentimental value was such that they considered it worth the effort of transporting it and its medieval ammunition across country and then installing it outside Kut, where it fired two ceremonial rounds every morning for some weeks! Each discharge was signalled by a peculiar and quite distinctive 'boom' which led to it being nicknamed by us 'Fanny', linked with an appropriate but vulgar adjective! If visibility was good and you were looking in the right direction you could see the great shell arcing up and then hurtling down followed by a faint trail of smoke from its time fuse. It landed with a great bump and a bounce, and after an unpredictable interval, would usually explode, scattering fragments of assorted metal, nails and stones lavishly around, rarely hitting anyone.

Our regimental lines were nearly a mile outside the town which meant that we could listen unmoved to the daily shelling, which normally followed a regular pattern, and could be turned to our advantage. Because I went to help at the General Hospital in Kut daily, I used to wait at a certain spot in the main communication trench for a suitable interval between salvos. On one of these journeys, turning the corner in a zigzag trench, I came upon an officer I knew lying on his back and, on examining him, found he was dead. Finding neither wound nor blood, I undid his jacket and found a small hole in it and an equally insignificant wound over the apex of his heart, evidently caused by a spent bullet. I could not help wondering what freak of fate had caused him to be killed here by a stray bullet and yet had favoured me at Ctesiphon.

Our nearest neighbours in the line were some Indian Sappers and Miners but we were only in touch via a rather roundabout communication trench. When things were quiet, we had an arrangement with their officers for a daily game of bridge and, if there was no sniping, we would risk a sprint across the open ground and then make a rapid dive into their Mess dugout. One day one of my colleagues got a bullet through his leg from a vigilant Turkish sniper, and although the rest of us treated the incident with unseemly hilarity, for a week or so we consented to go round the long, safe trench route.

About the middle of January we had several days of heavy rain and cold winds. The marshes and all low-lying ground became flooded and the water invaded the trenches and dugouts of both armies, making life very uncomfortable all round. The River Tigris then added to the misery by rising several feet, though at least this rendered us much safer from Turkish assault.

These floods very severely affected the progress of the Relieving Force. Up to now I have optimistically referred to it as the Relieving Force, but in view of its failure to relieve us, it has since been referred to as the Relief Force! The Turks had manned several lines of defence of great strength on both sides of the Tigris, utilizing several ridges in the area below Kut and using the floods and marshes in front of them as protection. It is certain that General Townshend must be held largely responsible for the disastrous losses suffered by the Relief Force because they felt obliged to respond to the petulant and peevish urgency of his appeals for relief, as a result of which troops of the force were flung piecemeal into battle without a proper build-up. Some delay could well have been acceptable as, at this stage, our situation was not critical. On such occasions we could hear the distant roar of artillery barrages indicating that an attack was in progress and at night see in which section of the sky the flashes of gunfire lay. Our spirits would then rise in anticipation of early relief, only to hear, when the noise of battle had died down, that there had been yet another costly setback, when gloom and disappointment would descend upon us once again.

The floods may have also been responsible for our inertia in the matter of launching demonstrations outside our perimeter, which, properly coordinated, might have provided significant diversions to aid the Relief Force. For, up to the middle of March, we in Kut were in pretty good shape physically and, if properly organized and led, could have sallied out and put up a stout show for a limited time and over a short distance. The diary again:

28 January. Siege conditions now well established. ------We have almost finished eating the great white bullocks that pulled the big 5 inch guns and shall be eating horse flesh in a day or two. The rain has been awful and we have had a really hard time, with everything getting flooded. Both the Turks and ourselves were flooded out of the frontline trench system and they have fallen right back, so that we enjoy greater peace. We had to go out each night in support in case of attack and got thoroughly wet and chilled, a foot deep in mud and water, incessant rain and a bitter wind blowing, so you can imagine what sort of a night we spent. ...I escaped with the complete loss of my voice. ...We can hear the Relief Force guns thundering away sixteen miles off, but they don't get any nearer. ...Neuman was hit again, in the shoulder this time, and I took the bullet out under 'local'. Playing bridge has been a great stand-by and we have whiled away many a long hour. We get up at 0830 hrs after cocoa and a biscuit, breakfast at 0930 hrs, bridge 1200 to 1400 hrs and again before dinner which is at 1830 hrs. Bed at 2100 hrs sharp. ...Food is now getting an acute problem. I killed our last chicken yesterday to forestall it being stolen. Sugar ration is one teaspoon each per day. Luckily I have some jam and tinned meat saved up so my Mess is not entirely dependent on ration issue. Bread is twelve ounces and meat eight ounces.

The Signal Corps erected a radio communication post in Kut using the field set which had been carried by mule transport throughout the campaign. The set worked with remarkable efficiency under difficult conditions although its range was limited to signals to and from a more powerful station down river. Through it we got Reuter's news each day which was widely circulated throughout the garrison and, when things were slack, a few personal messages were accepted for transmission. It was rumoured that much of the sets operating time was taken up by signals not unconnected with Townshend's personal interests and ambitions! One of my brothers [editor's note: Charles, the father of the narrative's editor] was the MO with the Manchester Regiment fighting down river in the Relief Force and I was able to send him a signal and learning in return that he had been slightly wounded but was still with his unit. (See Appendix 1.) The Reuter bulletins were not reassuring. The terrible losses on the Somme were hinted at and we learnt that there had been disasters in Serbia which had released a lot of Turkish and some German troops to reinforce the Turkish Army on our front, where the old German General von der Goltz had taken charge in Baghdad.

Chapter Nine

March and April 1916 in Kut

There were, by now, two topics of conversation in Kut, to the exclusion of almost all else: food and the progress of the Relief Force. The probable date of our relief was hotly debated and a number of bets and sweepstakes were arranged about it. Devising exotic menus for future meals had to be discouraged as it made the gastric juices flow too freely but none of us could disguise our hankering for unobtainable items, especially chocolates.

With the Indian troops, food became a more serious and urgent problem, their caste prejudices bedevilling all attempts at persuasion. Many castes never eat meat, obtaining their necessary animal protein from milk, which had ceased to be an item of ordinary ration or purchase, being strictly reserved for the hospitals. For meat eaters, mule was preferred to horse and we found camel sweetish and not too tough. Donkey, if young, was pronounced delicious but all these took a lot of disguising once our supply of curry powder and sauces came to an end. All slaughtering was done at a central depot, and when an officer's charger became a victim, the Mess in question had the melancholy privilege of claiming the tongue and heart, by far the most acceptable items for the table.

The long heated argument with the sepoys over the meat question was partially resolved by reference to various religious leaders in India, but some still remained to be persuaded. I was called one night to a young sepoy who had put the muzzle of his loaded rifle against his stomach and discharged it with his toe.

The result was as if he had swallowed a bomb, literally blowing himself to pieces.

Tobacco was another of our problems. Most Messes began with a good stock of pipe tobacco, cheroots and cigarettes, and some officers had private hoards, but official issues became meagre and soon ceased altogether. Some of the troops who felt the need to puff something were reduced to mixing well-used tea leaves with a pinch of ginger. Other substitutes also had their advocates.

When an officer died, his kit was sold at auction and there was always keen competition to buy any tobacco or cigarettes in it, for we all had plenty of money and nothing to spend it on. I bought for our Mess 100 cigarettes for 100 rupees (£6 12 shillings) which even at present prices seems a lot. For many weeks I was able to supplement Mess rations with extra items from our stock or by barter with other Messes: tinned bacon for whisky, or jam for biscuits. Each of us had our little 1 pound tin which he brought to meals and jealously took back to his dugout, it being human nature that one is more economical in consuming one's own small supply of sugar or jam. Near the end of the siege to celebrate someone's birthday, which coincided with a sudden burst of optimism over a bombardment heard down river, I produced, to general surprise and acclamation, a seven pound jar of jam, our last, and doled out a pound to each of our seven officers. There were also two tins of snails, 'escargot', which had remained neglected at the bottom of a Mess box. This esoteric delicacy was produced as a surprise and found takers. The beer barrel was empty and the Mess whisky finished. Our resident cat still slept in the niche in the Mess wall which housed the barrel, sustained by mice and any small birds I was able to shoot for it.

At that time, the importance of vitamins in the diet was only partially appreciated, except by most of the doctors, and evidence of the beginnings of certain deficiency diseases was appearing, especially amongst some castes of the Indian troops. About the end of February I noticed early signs of scurvy in some of my sepoys and not long afterwards cases of beri-beri began to be diagnosed among the British troops. A demonstra-

71

tion to illustrate these cases was held at the General Hospital in the town and a discussion followed. I pointed out that all over the open plain, within the defended area, a good crop of young herbs and grasses was growing after the rain and it was suggested that if the troops could be induced to gather and eat these herbs the problem of scurvy might be much eased. I broached the subject to our Colonel but, with his customary caution, he would not sanction the proposal, holding that men straying about the 'maidan' would be sniped at, although the nearest Turks were by now at least half a mile distant.

A few days later I alarmed him by reporting a serious increase in cases of scurvy, showing him some cases, and telling him that in a few days half his battalion would become unfit for duty. He then gave permission for scattered parties to go out and gather these herbs ('sag'), the sepoys taking up the idea with enthusiasm. Almost next day I met two of our sepoys carrying a huge cooking pot full of a variety of herbs which they said, in reply to my enquiry, was just for a few of their friends. There were one or two minor cases of upset tummies from eating unsuitable herbs but the men were pretty knowledgeable in such matters. The practice spread widely and we cautiously tried the mixed herbs in the Mess as a sort of spinach. In the regiment the result was quite remarkable. Fresh cases of scurvy ceased and, by the end of the siege, the worst cases had become of trivial importance and were no longer debilitating.

The first British aeroplane appeared over Kut on 3 February and was followed on the 11th by the first, and most unwelcome, visit from 'Fritz'. It was most unfortunate that in those days aeroplanes were so unreliable, at least so far as our experiences in Mesopotamia were concerned, nor had they in any way been adapted for the different jobs they were called upon to attempt. Flying was none too safe even without the additional hazard of flying over enemy territory. At Ctesiphon one of our pilots, the well known Bengal Lancer Yates-Brown, was sent to cut the telegraph line near Baghdad, but on landing on the rough desert the machine unluckily collided with one of the telegraph poles and he and his observer were captured, barely avoiding being shot by fellahin during their attempted flight on foot.

At Kut, the Turks had several aircraft and one German pilot, 'Fritz', who carried out bombing raids at no great height. We soon learnt to recognize his plane and how we hated the sight! You could clearly see the six bombs being released one by one and hear them whining down. You felt that number three, four and five had your name on them, more especially as the line of explosions on the ground seemed to confirm the probability. It gave one a helpless feeling of vulnerability which one could do nothing about.

The only relief we got was from watching the efforts of an improvised anti-aircraft gun, a well worn 15-pounder left behind by the Royal Horse Artillery and mounted on a wheel turntable contrivance. How we all wanted to pull the firing lanyard. Optimistically we gazed upwards and took heart to see the puff of white smoke indicating the shrapnel burst even though it never registered so much as a near miss. The other Turkish pilots were amateurs compared with Fritz and several of their planes came to grief or failed to become airborne on the plain to our north.

The Relief Force, down river, was terribly short of serviceable planes and at one time was said to have only one capable of taking the air. On their occasional flights over Kut the pilots dropped special items, important or privileged mail, newspapers and rubber gloves for the surgeons, but owing to their inexperience, the strong winds and the small landing area available, several loads fell into the river or into Turkish hands. At least we appreciated their efforts. Life in Kut by the end of February was dull with very little military activity apparent or possible, and with a steadily falling standard of living, making us critical and peevish. It was a wonder that we kept on good terms with each other.

At the beginning of March we learnt that the Relief Force, under a succession of generals, had reached a point where they could launch an attack on the strongly defended final Turkish position at Es Sinn, only ten miles down river from us at Kut. The Turks were strongly established on both sides of the Tigris, their right flank consisting of a system of trenches, the Dujaila Redoubt. They had a boat bridge and a flying ferry but the great bulk of their forces was on the left bank.

The Relief Force attack was made at dawn on 8 March up the right bank of the river and it took the Turks by surprise. The leading British troops got right up to the Redoubt and reported that much of it appeared to be unoccupied. I heard this fully confirmed from Turkish sources some months later as a captive in Baghdad. It would appear that our troops could not only have carried the Redoubt but could have swept right by, rendering our relief almost certain. Alas, the golden chance was thrown away! The infantry in front of Dujaila were ordered to halt and dig in pending artillery support and proper reconnaissance. Meanwhile the Turks rushed troops pell-mell across the river and into the empty trenches, with the result that when the assault was finally sanctioned it was beaten off with such heavy losses that the whole force had to retire to a former position several miles back to reorganize. The last real chance of relief had gone. Would the generals never learn to allow, and encourage, local initiative?

On this occasion we in Kut showed some enterprise in a belated effort to contribute to our own deliverance. A small mobile force of selected soldiers and sepoys was collected in a palm grove on the river bank below Kut town ready at the right moment to embark in three or four dhows and launches and then be ferried across the Tigris under covering fire with the objective of making a vigorous thrust in the direction of the rear of the Dujaila Redoubt. I was a member of this commando-type group and was glad of the chance to take part in a dangerous enterprise, being tired of inaction.

We remained ready for instant action from 0300 hrs till after midday awaiting the signal to move, listening hopefully to the distant battle and were even able to see the dust of moving columns of troops, but gradually the firing grew weaker and finally died down. In the evening, instead of effecting a triumphal and emotional meeting with the Relief Force out on the plain south of the Hai, we returned to our unit lines in the spring sunshine bitter and disconsolate and back to the prolonged frustration of idleness and inaction.

I do not think that our little commando waiting in the palm grove was as secret and well-concealed as it should have been for, during our vigil, we were suddenly subjected to a burst of shrapnel shells from a new quick-firing battery, said to have been fired from British guns captured in the Dardanelles, but more probably German or Austrian guns. In any case, it was a nasty experience, subjecting us to shell bursts before we heard the gun report, unlike the more gentlemanly Turkish batteries to which we were accustomed, where on hearing the four distant reports of gun fire we had time to take cover before the shells arrived.

Immediately after the Dujaila fiasco our rations were heavily cut. At the same time, many of the Arabs left in Kut began trying to get away at night in small boats or by swimming or floating on inflated skins; a poor prospect in either case. As at Es Sinn, the Turks now greatly strengthened the trench system facing the Relief Force, and to make matters worse, rain caused flooding in the low-lying ground over which the force had to make its advance. The frontal assaults repeatedly failed, at fearful cost, the infantry struggling through tenacious mud which clogged their rifle barrels and even their mouths when they fell. In all the force lost 22,000 men in its efforts to get through to us. The Relief Force had done all that was possible, and more.

For the next month nothing much happened in Kut. We were steadily losing physical condition as a result of the repeated reduction in rations. An atmosphere of gloom pervaded the place. Our big 5-inch guns engaged the Turkish ferry at Megassis but as it was only just within range they could not hope to do much damage. And I, for my part, let off steam by shooting a few sparrows for our cat!

2 April, 1916. They talk of sending our mails in by aeroplane which they might have done weeks ago, but as they have already dropped one bag in the river, one would rather wait. The parcels weigh eighty lbs and have two white sheets attached so that they do not fall too fast and can be easily seen. One has just fallen, a good shot this time, though it fell with a great splash in 'casual water'.

5 April. Getting near the end now. The siege must end one way or the other by about the 16 April and if Gorringe fails

I shall have to tear up my letters and papers and prepare to march to Mosul (prophetic words)! ... Gorringe made a big attack at dawn today. We heard a violent bombardment, all his guns going hard for an hour and a half and then silence.

13 April. Things are getting rather desperate. We only get five oz of bread each day which it would be quite easy to finish off at breakfast though the only thing left to eat with it is anchovy sauce!...The tommies ration is bread, chiefly barley, with about one and a half lbs of horse or mule, with a pinch of salt, recalling memories of Barlash of the Guards. ...My daily walk into town to help the hospital makes me quite tired now. I have to take a rest half way. Our bread finishes on 21 April unless they cut it down once more, but we could hold on a bit after that I suppose if need be on a diet of mule and grass. General Houghton, who led our column at Ctesiphon, died yesterday and we gave him a big funeral. He had been upset by the siege diet and died of acute enteritis.

Bread was now issued in the form of little 10 oz loaves, one for every two individuals, and its exact division became the object of jealous scrutiny. The procedure commonly adopted was for one participant to cut it in two and the other to choose his half! It became an anxious test of judgement and steadiness of hand. I was regarded, by virtue of my profession, as an expert.

Although the outlook had become quite desperate as regards the prospect of relief, we clutched at a ray of hope in mid-April when planes began to drop food into Kut. It took the form of huge double sacks of flour, lentils or sugar enclosed in loose covers to save the contents if they burst on hitting the ground. It was quite a sight to see the great white shining bundles come hurtling down and some very optimistic estimates were made as to how this strategy would affect our chances of holding out. My own opinion, as recorded in my diary, was 'they would have to drop at least 15,000 lbs a day to keep us going (which they cannot hope to do) and I fancy that the idea is just to help us hang on for a few extra days'.

Each aeroplane was only able to make one drop per day of 240 – 300 lbs. This historic effort to keep us going was started much too late and proved to be sadly inadequate despite the great endeavours of the gallant pilots.

However, not known to us until the last possible moment for security reasons, there was one more desperate throw of the dice to be made. The fine river steamer *Julnar* was at Amara undergoing an overhaul. She was selected to attempt to run through the Turkish positions with a full month's supply of food for the garrison. All was to be done in the greatest secrecy but it was obvious that the secret would leak out in Amara and the intention and destination of the ship known or guessed by the Turks. Indeed it would have been very difficult to disguise the project because the work of fixing heavy steel plates around the bridge and engine room and loading on board all sorts of food could not be concealed from the local labour force employed.

In more modern times (1949), HMS *Amethyst*, a modern ship, made a brilliant escape down the wide Yangtse River. In 1916 the old *Julnar* was asked to attempt the heroic task of passing up the Tigris, against the current, through a specially prepared defensive position at a range of 100 yards, an impossible mission virtually doomed to tragic failure from the start.

This most dangerous, even reckless, enterprise was undertaken as a matter of course by the Royal Navy. Lieutenant Firman RN was given command in association with our dear friend and famous river pilot, Charley Cowley, who had been given a commission in the RNVR. Cowley knew only too well that he was regarded as a Turkish subject and therefore as a traitor by the Turks and could expect no mercy if captured. Volunteering for the task of piloting the *Julnar* on its fantastic voyage was in itself an act of outstanding courage but was fully in character with his swashbuckling reputation. About a dozen naval ratings formed the crew, all volunteers.

By the night of 24 April 1916 the heavily laden ship was ready and she moved off upstream at her best speed. An artillery barrage and heavy machine-gun and rifle fire was kept up by the British forces on both banks to distract attention and to try to mask the sound of the ships engines. Even our old 5-inch

77

guns loosed off in the general direction of the rear of the Turkish position, without the gunners knowing the reason for doing so. The *Julnar* reached the Turkish frontline undetected but probably not unexpected, for there were Arab spies everywhere.

Immediately an intense hail of rifle bullets was directed at her, clattering against her sides. I was told that the firing directed across the river, when it missed the *Julnar*, probably hit some of their own troops on the other bank, but this consideration did not weigh very heavily with the Turkish troops! Perhaps the inaccuracy of their aim may be excused because of the heavy fire directed at them from the *Julnar* itself and from their comrades on the other bank.

Passing miraculously right through the Sannaiyat position, she then came under fire from their artillery at point blank range but still held her course in spite of Lieutenant Firman being killed on the bridge and several members of the crew being wounded. Cowley, although himself wounded managed to keep her going and it appeared indeed possible that she might get clear through and reach Kut but, alas, when she came up to the Turkish ferry at Megassis her screws and rudder got fouled by a cable running across the river at that point. She came to a stop, swung onto a sandbank, failed in her efforts to break clear and was captured.

Cowley was taken before a Turkish officer on shore, recognized and shot out of hand. This I learned in Baghdad a few months later from an authority I regard as reliable. Nothing was ever known officially about his fate, or how his body was disposed of, but according to the British sailors he was not killed on the ship. The ratings were taken away as prisoners to a camp right up in Anatolia. Firman and Cowley were each awarded posthumous Victoria Crosses.

The news that an attempt to 'run the blockade' was being made became known in our Mess late that night and once more we were cheered by a gleam of hope, only to have it extinguished when, in the first light of dawn on 25 April, we saw in the distance across the plain of Megassis the gallant ship, stationary and with no sign of movement on board, nor of smoke coming from her funnel.

The last hope had gone. It was at once announced that General Townshend had been told to open negotiation with the Turkish commander, Khalil Pasha, to arrange terms for our surrender. The bitter, but inevitable, truth had at last to be faced. The garrison at Kut had held out longer than that at Ladysmith, but it was all in vain.

Chapter Ten

The Surrender of Kut

Vae Victis, Woe to the Conquered
'By the Waters of Babylon We Sat Down and Wept'

I was standing on the bank of the river next morning when I saw our only serviceable launch proceeding upstream flying a large white flag. A temporary ceasefire had been proclaimed and a most unusual silence prevailed. We were all glad and took advantage of it to get ourselves and our possessions out into the open. I even tried a short swim, quite a thrill in spite of the sticky mud at the edge of the water.

It was Townshend in the launch, accompanied by a couple of staff officers, and they were on their way to the Turkish camp at Shamran to negotiate surrender on the best terms they could get. He was almost unknown to us by sight, not like his brigadiers who correctly cultivated acquaintance with the ranks. Latterly there had been some talk of minor dissension amongst the brigadiers over questions connected with the regular assumption of frontline duties. Townshend had let it be known, or understood, that his health had become indifferent and this may well have been so. However, some officers were somewhat cynical when reading his long and frequent communiqués and exhortations issued alike to us and the Relief Force.

I must especially mention one of our Brigade Commanders, Major General Melliss, who was always most popular with and helpful to the troops, notably during the terrible march of the men of the garrison as prisoners of war up to Anatolia. Melliss had gained a VC in the South African War in 1900. If he had a failing, it was in lack of tact in dealing with our captors, who refused to be bullied out of their easy-going ways.

It was hoped that surrender terms would allow all Indian troops to return to India, under parole not to fight against Turkey, but this condition could not possibly have been accepted by the Turks, even when sugared by the offer of a large sum as ransom. However the Turks did agree that the sick could be left in Kut and then later taken down river for handing over to the Relief Force. This concession was not made on purely humanitarian motives but rather to relieve the Turks of the burden of their care and treatment. They were to be exchanged for an equal number of healthy Turkish soldiers (not Arabs) held as prisoners by us. In all other respects it was unconditional surrender and the 29 April was fixed as the mournful day. We had existed for the last week on our emergency rations and on food dropped by aeroplane, only a ration of 4 oz of flour or biscuit, about 6 oz of mule meat and a morsel of chocolate.

The 29 April broke calm and sunny, with a light cool breeze. Under happier circumstances it might have been a day to rejoice the heart but for us it was a day of heartbreak. The siege had lasted for five months and, although we had in our regimental lines quite a number of fairly fit but thin sepoys, the garrison had latterly only been able to undertake purely routine defensive duties.

Down in the battered town and in the hospitals the picture was appalling. The weather by day was now very hot and on entering the town one was met by an all-pervading, sickening stench. Sanitation had never been properly organized and the normal open spaces for such primitive needs not being available, filth accumulated and rotted everywhere. Dysentery, fever, anaemia and tuberculosis were carrying off twenty men a day; men already weakened by starvation, malaria, scurvy and beri-beri, their gums oozing pus, their cheeks sunken, with every rib outlined and legs and feet misshapen with dropsy and without even the spirit to beat off the flies that swarmed about them. It was heartrending for us, the devoted medical staffs, who were helpless and felt we had lost our own special battle. It was a pitiful sight to see previously robust and cheerful men reduced to such misery and distress, too often with a look of resigned despair in their eyes.

> Lonely ones, you do not walk alone.
> Nor lonely do you suffer your pain.
> We walk beside you.

Never shall I forget that morning of surrender. It must live vividly in the memory of each one of us who was there. But first, before the entry of the Turks, it was necessary to distribute the cash in the field treasure chest and everyone received, roughly according to his rank, a small sum in gold and rupees. After that we settled down to the melancholy task of destruction. Everywhere you looked you saw columns of smoke rising into the clear sky as piles of saddlery, broken mule carts and every variety of equipment of potential use to the enemy was burnt; the flames being fed with matting, fodder, empty boxes and surplus firewood. Rifle bolts, ammunition and shells were dumped in the river, all rifles smashed but for a few kept as self defence against possible Arab miscreants in the town.

The whole plain resounded with the distinctive sharp metallic explosions made by blowing up all the guns. Poor Gunners! Some of them were in tears as the guns which they were so proud to have served and tended were filled with guncotton and blown to pieces. I was particularly sorry for the Volunteer Battery, manned by Eurasians from Calcutta, such a gallant, friendly lot and so devoted to the 'motherland' they had never seen. This Battery was nicknamed the 'Buchanans', the Black and White Battery, after a well known brand of whisky, but it was an affectionate nickname.

Soon after midday we saw a Turkish column marching in along the loop of the river by the fort, headed by an officer on a horse. We stood at our bivouacs, by the smouldering heaps, while Turkish detachments came, in an orderly manner but rather self-consciously, to take charge of each unit, guided by our own people.

They were the swarthy, stocky Anatolian types we came to know so well later, wearing full field kit with heavy packs. Their greenish-brown uniform showed signs of hard service and their footwear was strangely assorted but practical. For headdress they wore the folding cloth, enveriya, introduced by Enver Pasha at the time of the Balkan Wars. The officers wore an upright cap of astrakhan, the kalpak, with radiating stripes of gold or silver braid across the crown.

The senior Turkish Colonel who rode in to take our surrender from General Townshend was extremely angry to find that we had blown up all our guns, the capture of which in those days carried a lot of prestige. As a matter of fact, all our guns were pretty well worn out, in addition to which the Turks would have had great difficulty in finding ammunition for them. Several of the guns were quite obsolete.

The Turkish 'nefers' seemed quite embarrassed by their role but were well behaved. In the town a few cases of attempted robbery occurred, but when resisted, the offenders did not persist and on complaint being made to a Turkish officer, the offender was promptly and severely dealt with.

Whilst none of us at this time suffered any ill-treatment and very few were robbed, it was a very different fate that befell the local inhabitants. All their goods and personal possessions were confiscated or looted and a terrible revenge was taken against all who had helped us, or were suspected of having helped us. The Sheik of Kut and a wealthy and important Jewish banker named Sassoon and several others, interpreters and the like, were all hanged together on one long gallows in the centre of the wrecked town. Others were shot out of hand and some escaped after being severely beaten up. Those who tried to escape down river were easily caught and brought back. There were Turkish and Arab traitors in the town who readily betrayed the victims, guided by an intelligence system that had, for centuries, enabled the Turks to maintain hold over their ramshackle empire.

One memory of that last evening in Kut was seeing our poor *Firefly*, all gaily dressed up with bunting and flags, and with a smart Turkish crew at attention on deck and the Turkish flag at her stern, steam in triumph into Kut with our chief captor Khalil Pasha on board. (The *Firefly*, together with the *Sumara*, was recaptured by General Maude's army many months later just north of where she had been lost and Lieutenant Commander Eddis RN, who had commanded her, was re-appointed to command her.) This was a bitter sight for our few naval personnel and for Tudway RN who had to hand over his battle-scarred *Sumara* that same day.

And so ended the long weary Siege of Kut, which had lasted for 147 days. We did not imagine on that day what horrors still lay ahead and how few of us would survive the next two and a half years of captivity.

The last entry in my siege diary reads:

29 April 1916. We blew up our 40 guns today and burnt everything of any military value. I fired my revolver into the prisms of my beautiful binoculars, then smashed the revolver with a sledge hammer, burnt my saddlery and threw my sword into the Tigris. ---(we had long since eaten my poor old grey charger) ---we are now all camped along the river edge and Turkish river boats have come to take boat loads of prisoners during the night to their main camp up river.

My diary was smuggled out and, with other of my letters and papers, is now in the Imperial War Museum.

Kut had fallen at last and we were 'in the bag'. I do not think that at first we realized the full enormity of the disaster that had befallen us. We had become bored with the inaction during the final few weeks of the dreary siege, contributed to by a sense of sadness and disappointment that all the efforts and sacrifices of the Relief Force had been in vain. But at the same time there was some feeling of relief (if in this context so incongruous a word can be used) that the period of inaction was over, that there would be at least a change of scene with, we hoped, a more peaceful background. Hardship, no doubt, but with fresh interests to engage one's attention.

I believe that nearly all of us underestimated the perils and hardships which lay ahead. On the day we capitulated 11 per cent of the Garrison were in hospital, and many more would require building up before they could be expected to face the very long desert and mountain march ahead of them, 1,200 miles in the burning heat of May, June and July. The end result was that of 12,000 or so British and Indian troops who were taken into captivity by the Turks, at least 4,000 died. The British fared much the worst. About 2,600 British officers and other ranks became prisoners but only 700 returned two and a half years later at the end of the war. Now, a mere handful of those are still alive [ed. written in about 1970].

The 9,500 Indians fared better. They had been recruited from Indian villages where food was simple, largely vegetarian, and needed little preparation and where footwear, if worn at all, was primitive and practical. They were therefore able to adapt much more easily to the conditions prevailing on the appalling up-country march which destroyed their British comrades. India was, of course, not divided at that time into India, Pakistan and Bangladesh. As for the British, throughout the desert marches and in the final camps the officers suffered much less severely than the rank and file and their survival rate was much higher. Also, we had been generally in better shape at the end of the siege. Our Messes had been able to maintain a small extra ration almost to the end to supplement the official ration. As a class we had the advantage of a better education and perhaps more self-control and intellectual resource and, a most important point, a certain amount of money, including a slightly higher share of the field treasure chest distributed at the end of the siege. The troops were used to being provided with all their basic needs and were inclined to regard any loose cash as to be spent on their fancies or urges of the moment, without regard to the desperate hardships ahead.

It is known that at least one soldier, overcome by hunger and having run out of small change and negotiable articles of clothing and kit, gave an Arab in a village a golden sovereign for a couple of local loaves and a hunk of dates. Such were the straits to which many men were reduced. Others were wiser and these stood a better chance of coming through. There were:

> …those who husbanded the Golden Grain
> and those who flung it to the winds like rain.

85

But this is looking far ahead and we are immediately concerned with the evacuation of Kut.

The day following the capitulation, under Turkish orders, most of the officers and some of the more debilitated troops (apart from those selected by Turkish doctors to be invalided down river, numbering some 1,500 of which, for political reasons, the majority were Mohammedans), together with our orderlies and some Indian servants, were taken up in steamers and barges to the Turkish camp at Shumran. However, under pressure from the local Turkish commander, who pleaded shortage of coal, most of the men were made to march the nine miles to the camp. This resulted in many men failing to make it there, some dying on the track whilst others struggled in to Shumran in a state of collapse, arriving more hungry and exhausted than ever, the symptoms of dysentery and the terrible starvation diarrhoea becoming evident.

At Shumran, a great pile of Turkish army biscuits was made available. These extraordinary objects deserve special mention. They looked like large round dog biscuits of the coarser kind and were incredibly hard and dry. You could scarcely break them with a hammer, but they had the unexpected property that when heated they became flexible and small pieces could be twisted off and chewed. They could also be rendered into a most unpalatable gruel by prolonged boiling but unfortunately they contained so much dirt, husk and extraneous matter that it required a powerful and unimpaired digestion to cope with them. Consequently, they proved to be a fatal diet for our unfortunate British troops, although the Indians seemed better able to prepare a meal from them.

To add to this problem, the only source of drinking and cooking water was the Tigris, dirty and polluted, with the immediate result that a virulent epidemic of choleric dysentery broke out. There were no hospitals or drugs and it was a pitiful sight to see the wretched men making their way, sometimes dragging themselves along on hands and knees, to the latrine trenches, there to be overwhelmed by legions of flies. Nearly all of us became affected to a greater or lesser extent and the symptoms persisted for weeks after. Our field hospitals and their doctors had remained behind in Kut to dispose of the siege patients and the few sanitary or nursing orderlies with us were mostly in as bad a state as their patients. No less than 300 men died at that camp during the first week and many who made a recovery, or tried to make it appear so, soon relapsed with this terrible starvation dysentery which slowly weakened them so that at some point on the interminable desert march before them, in tropical summer heat, they fell out on the track and died. Failing that, they were left behind at some wretched Arab hut on the outskirts of a village, overwhelmed in squalor and despair and often dying alone at the last.

The Relief Force sent up to us by arrangement with the Turks, two barges of supplies and rations, mails and Mess stores, which would have been valuable beyond price if they had arrived and been distributed quickly. However, Turkish methods were dilatory in the extreme. After many delays they adopted the obvious policy of leaving it to us to handle the distribution problem. Unfortunately at that early stage we were not organized to cope with such a task, particularly as parties of our band were already being sent up river, on steamers if they were lucky, otherwise again on foot, with scarcely a chance of enjoying any of the good and lifesaving things dumped higgledy-piggledy on the river bank.

It is an accepted principle in dealing with prisoners of war to separate the officers from their men. The Turks did this despite our protests and they continued this practice throughout our captivity. The intention of this practice was to ensure that the men, deprived of the support and guidance of their trusted officers, became more amenable to Turkish discipline and control. It has been said that on this occasion we 'abandoned' our men. Nothing could be further from the truth and there were countless incidents on the march up country when officers individually or collectively rescued and sustained unfortunate men found in distress, using their own carefully saved money to procure food, shelter and transport for them. General Melliss and Padre Spooner were outstanding in showing what could be done to help the helpless, even under conditions of the greatest difficulty.

The first move north from Shumran was made on the night of 4 May when a party of 100 British officers, including myself, with a number of Indian officers and orderlies, found ourselves on board a Turkish steamer bound for Baghdad. There was, as usual, a barge tied on each side. One side was full of Turkish wounded; the other carried a damaged aircraft for repair or overhaul. We camped down with our possessions on the deck of the little vessel, soon so overcrowded that it was almost impossible to move without stepping upon someone or some chattel. Gradually a sort of orderliness grew out of the chaos helped by the fact that some provident members had the presence of mind to grab a few items of edible rations. We spent most of the time eating or sleeping on deck just where we had settled ourselves. Little groups formed and they remained together as travelling units for the rest of the weeks ahead. Each person made his individual contribution of specialized skill or equipment, placing it at the service of the rest of the group, not the least of which was the understanding and good humour arising from close association. Discomfort was thus diminished and even the medieval sanitary arrangements and the stifling midday heat and smells became endurable.

We steamed forlornly past well-remembered spots where we had advanced so full of hope and eagerness six months before and had subsequently seen again on our fighting retreat – Aziziyeh, Lejj and its woods, High Wall and Ctesiphon, the Great Arch with the little village of Sulman Pak under its shade, the objective of our attack that we failed to capture on that tragic November day. Our thoughts went back to our lost regiment and forward to the inevitable hardships our poor sepoys would be facing during the coming months.

Distressfully I tried to get a view of the site of the Water Redoubt where our own Major Riddell had fallen and where he forever lies, attended by the youthful Venis and so many of his sepoys. (Survivors of his company of sepoys of the 48th Pioneers, on returning to India in 1919 named one of their villages 'Riddellpore' in token of their devotion to his memory.) And as we steamed away north, there was a feeling that we had deserted them, lying in a shallow unmarked grave in a hostile land.

Gliding past each village, we were mocked and jeered at by the river Arabs; we had not yet got used to enduring these indignities and humiliations, or worse atrocities, that some of these treacherous people delighted to inflict upon us. The women sent up an ululating chorus of triumph and the small boys made obscene and insulting gestures, running along the bank to keep up with the steamer as it chugged by and drawing their fingers significantly across their throats.

Soon after passing the mouth of the Diyala River, coming in from the Persian side, we began to perceive the outlines of the minarets and domes of the famous old city we had attempted so rashly to capture. We steamed past tropical gardens and orchards seeing houses of increasing size on the left bank of the Tigris. The larger houses, well built of brick and stone, all flew the Red Crescent flag showing that they had been taken over as hospitals. We stopped at one of these while the barge containing the sick and wounded was detached and moored. The finest building, the former British Consulate, which had been converted to an officers' hospital, was another stopping place. Here we saw a number of German nurses in nuns' clothing moving about.

Finally on that morning of 9 May we tied up at a good brick and timber quay near the centre of the city, some 500 miles up the Tigris from Basra, under the interested and not always hostile gaze of a group of inhabitants of diverse races. Despite the discomforts and distresses of the five day voyage, we were already feeling rested, were less desperate with hunger and more competent to cope with whatever the future might have in store for us. It was just as well that we had built up a little reserve of strength, for we still had before us all the trials of a most formidable desert march and 1,000 mile journey to our prisoner of war camps away across the Toros Mountains in Anatolia.

On disembarking at Baghdad, we were formed into a marching column, senior officers being provided with 'phaetons' to ride in. The procession wound through the main streets, through the great historic bazaar and on to the cavalry barracks near the north gate of the city. En route we were subjected to insulting remarks and gestures by sections of the crowd but I got the impression that this conduct was officially organized rather than spontaneous and this impression was strengthened when I was in Baghdad again, alone this time, six months later.

The cavalry barracks was built on the usual eastern plan – a great open square entered into through a massive iron-studded wooden door. Inside all the rooms opened onto a wide first floor gallery facing the central courtyard. Below them were the horse stalls and storage sheds, all very stoutly built and, for a Turkish barracks, remarkably clean. We were allowed to divide up the available accommodation, the Indian officers naturally preferring to occupy one part whilst we took the other, our messing habits being so different.

A contractor provided us with two good meals a day, exactly the same, a meat stew with onions or beans, very greasy, followed by stuffed cucumber (kabak dolmasi) and yoghurt. It was a monotonous diet but, for us, very acceptable and satisfying. This cost us a mejidieh (four shillings) a day, a high price at the current market rates in a land of plenty. The contractor no doubt made a useful profit in spite of having to oil the palm of some official to get the contract. He then made some more by selling us fruit and local Arab cigarettes.

Next day we were allowed to visit the American Consul, the kind and helpful Mr Brissell, to whom all of us prisoners owed so much. He gave each of us a pound or two in Turkish gold and took our names so as to inform our families in England; a real kindness to them and us. Rather to our surprise, the Turks gave us an advance of pay to which we were after all entitled as prisoners of war. In my case, as a Subaltern, I got seven Turkish pounds (for a month), two of them in gold and five in the much depreciated paper currency. It was the last time I was paid in gold for soon all metallic money disappeared from circulation, being replaced by paper or even by very dirty postage stamps of the smallest denominations.

Baghdad in 1916 was almost unchanged from the days of Haroun al Raschid and I think that the great Caliph would have had little difficulty in finding his way along its covered bazaars and narrow alleys, guided by an occasional glimpse of the high domes and slender towering minarets of its many mosques, from which the muezzins called to the faithful from the four corners at the appropriate time to prostrate themselves in prayer. Some of the domes were dazzling, with glazed mosaics in lapis lazuli and white, others glittering with gold leaf. In the two or three short journeys we were able to make in Baghdad before we were sent north, such attention as we attracted was not hostile and often quite friendly. This was due to the large numbers of Christians of various sects and Jews mingling with the local Arabs in the streets and bazaars. They all wore costumes and distinctive fezzes or other headdress which indicated their race or country of origin, a refreshing habit compared with the drab uniformity of hats which nowadays seems to have replaced them universally.

The often flamboyant dresses of the men, especially of the few but conspicuous proud-striding Kurds, added greatly to the scene, with gay saddlebags and kilims draped over the camels, ponies and mules of the caravanserais. I do not recollect seeing a single motor vehicle and I prefer to remember Baghdad like that!

Chapter Eleven

Honoured Guests!

When Allah made hell he did not find it bad enough so he made
Mesopotamia; and then he added flies.

Arab Proverb

The question invariably asked of ex-prisoners of war of the
Turks is 'and how did they treat you?' A.J. Barker, in *The
Neglected War*, published in 1967, suggests that it was as bad as
under Genghis Khan and Tamerlane, but E.W.C. Sandes
probably gave a truer estimate in his book *In Kut and Captivity*,
published in 1919, himself one of the prisoners, when he wrote:

> The utter neglect shown to us officers by the Turks may be
> traced, not to ill-will, but to absolute apathy, dislike of
> responsibility and incompetence. Our captors were not cruel
> to us or even hostile but in most cases simply left us alone,
> neglecting all appeals for assistance.

Both views are supported by ample evidence and I can personally testify to both.

It was particularly unfortunate that at the very beginning of
our ordeal it was announced by the War Minister, Enver Pasha
himself, and repeated by our captor, the Turkish commander
Khalil Pasha, that we were to be Turkey's 'Honoured Guests', a
promise immediately forgotten by our hosts but ruefully
remembered and quoted by the 'guests' when their treatment at
the captors' hands was at its most callous and brutal. We quickly
became cynical and disillusioned over it.

It is true that one notable exception was made in favour of General Townshend who was sent forward with the minimum of delay to Constantinople, travelling with a special escort in VIP style, destined to live for the rest of the war in comparative comfort on an island in the sea of Marmora! The rest of us were not so lucky, and the inescapable fact remains that only one out of every four of the British who had been under his command survived their term of captivity. The number of Indians who returned to India was never known. Many of those unaccounted for were Mohammedans who had found little difficulty in melting away as religious pilgrims in a land where there were so many highly revered Holy Places of Islam, Kerbala, Nejef and Hilla for example, attracting annually large numbers of devout Moslems from India and neighbouring countries. Others escaped from working parties and took up local occupations in the cosmopolitan cities in Mesopotamia and Syria. This was not difficult as the Turks tended to give preferential treatment and extra liberties to their co-religionists.

In addition to money, there were qualities almost as important which were needed for survival as a prisoner of war; language, adaptability and cunning. All of these were of no avail if one's physical condition had fallen below the point of no return. Every prisoner of war in every war has learnt the value, the necessity, of being able to communicate with his captors. The Arab and Kurdish guard and escort who drove us on up to and beyond Mosul used words only for the purpose of impelling us on (yallah) or to forbidding us from some action (yassak). Senior officers, usually Turks, sometimes knew a little French. Turkish is a well constructed tongue, the elements of grammar of which were not difficult to acquire, and a study of it, when opportunity offered, enabled a prisoner to be not only helpful to his fellows but to be of use to Turkish officials, great and minor, in facilitating business, whether on the march or in camp. An accepted position as an intermediary might also gain the prisoner added status in the eyes of the Turkish lower ranks. Adaptability had come easily to most of us who came through imprisonment, supplemented on occasions by cunning and skulduggery when certain circumstances offered opportunity.

Sadly, for many, Baghdad was as far as they got on the road to captivity. Some died between Kut and Baghdad due to the great hardships of a march forced upon them in their weakened condition, compounded by shocking ill-treatment by the brutal escorts. Others were sorted out as a second batch of invalids to be sent back down river, accompanied by all the doctors of our military hospitals, unlike us regimental doctors who remained captives until the end of the war. This despite the fact that there was little we could do for our fellow prisoners owing to lack of suitable accommodation, drugs or equipment. I feel that we should have been sent back as soon as we had accompanied the various parties to the up-country camps, where we were far less useful than on the march or at the intermediate staging posts.

For my own party, there was to be no tarrying in Baghdad. On 12 May we were paraded, counted for the hundredth time, marched across the boat bridge to the railway station and entrained for Samarra. This short stretch of the Baghdad Railway, from Baghdad to Samarra, had recently been completed by the Germans with material brought from Basra by the river steamers. We junior officers were crowded into very definitely third-class carriages, senior officers doing rather better, whilst General Townshend had most of a carriage to himself, though none of us saw him. The rail journey, of only eighty miles, took five hours. The excessive heat was made far more unbearable by a violent dust storm, so that we reached Samarra in the evening tired, hot, and very dirty and of course, as usual, hungry. Hunger continued to nag us for several weeks after our prolonged period of starvation in Kut. The station, recognizable by a couple of small buildings and a lot of military dumps, was on the right bank a mile from the river, whilst the town was several miles away on the opposite bank. The Turkish officer in charge of us, one Elmi Bey, wanted to be bothered with us as little as possible and issued orders that we were to remain in our carriages all night. Naturally we took no notice of this and as soon as he had cleared off we spread ourselves around on what there was of a platform.

The great attraction there was a water standpipe and in time we all got a good drink and at least a partial wash before settling

94

down in our blankets or sleeping bags on the bare ground in the small groups into which we had already organized ourselves. My little party included Matthews, the Sapper, the hearty Matthias and our Adjutant, Burdett, who had brought along our old Mess cook, not for any benefit he could provide for us, but to try to save his life as he had lost several toes from trench foot in Kut and could only hobble along. We had some small bags of rations and he willingly contrived to cook us something in the couple of cooking pots we had brought.

We waited two or three days at Samarra station while transport was collected together for our 150 mile desert march to Mosul and spent the time bartering the surplus possessions we could carry no further, in exchange for flat wheaten cakes, water melons, dates, yoghurt and eggs. Finally, the transport turned out to be a number of droves of donkeys, most of them several degrees more miserable than G.K. Chesterton's donkey:

> ...tattered outlaw of the earth,
> Of ancient crooked will!

Their distribution presented Elmi with a problem he gladly handed over to us, as was his way when faced with any difficulty. The drovers each owned a variable number of donkeys and naturally insisted that all their donkeys, good and bad, must go on the long journey together. The allocation worked out at one donkey per officer, with no allowance for an orderly or servant who, in the Turkish Army, always carried his own kit from one stage to the next. Nobody was satisfied with this allocation but it was no good appealing to Elmi who could never be found on such occasions. He rode an Arab pony and had, I remember, formidable moustaches, but to us he was a useless character, without even proper control over our armed guard.

My little group got three good donkeys and one weakling but as I was to be rear of the column I was given, or wangled, a rather splendid grey donkey. Racing men may recall a Derby winner (I think in 1912) called Minoru, a grey, so of course this name was bestowed on this animal. Being easier to pick out at night, when we always completed our march, he helped many a sick man on to the next halt and even occasionally afforded me

95

a ride. Not that riding these sharp-backed animals was easy or comfortable, without saddle or stirrups. Even with feet trailing along the ground you felt you were being bisected by their sharp bony backs. The Arab boys had developed the knack of lying along the animal's back with an arm around its neck and even seemed able to sleep for hours like that! Each donkey had slung under its belly a goatskin of water and on its back we tied, or balanced precariously, such possessions as we had left, walking beside it or near it lest the load fell off or an attempt was made to steal it.

On account of the fierce heat of the sun, Elmi marched us by night which was, in theory, a good idea. The first night there was a full moon and, as the desert was smooth, marching was not difficult and a good pace was maintained much of the time. However, a few days later, with the moon waning and rising later each night and the track getting rougher and more irregular, it became very trying for us at the back of the dusty column. Elmi would call a halt every hour or so to enable the tail to catch up, when he would set off again, so that we poor tail-enders rarely got any worthwhile rest or even time to re-adjust loads. We stumbled along wearily hour after hour suffering in the dust and smell of those ahead instead of enjoying the cool fresh air enjoyed by those in the front of the column.

I acted as whipper-in all the way to Mosul with the stalwart help of the 'mad' Sapper. If a man fell out it was essential that he be brought on as otherwise the Arabs would strip him and leave him to die. One night we put an Indian who had collapsed on to Minoru's back and marched for hours holding him in a sitting position, one of us on each side. Because of the razor sharpness of the beast's back he kept slipping down one side or the other until, in desperation, we turned him face-down sideways across the beast's back and held him in the darkness until we finally halted, only to find him dead. For how long he had been dead we didn't know. We just had time to bury him in a shallow grave and then we were off again.

Water on the route in these marches was another difficulty. When we came to a stagnant pool of flood water the donkeys

96

would walk in and foul it in more ways than one. It required a powerful thirst to counterbalance the smell and the taste. We tail-enders again suffered the worst.

The first march of all, between Samarra and Tikrit, was by far the worst. It started in the evening of 15 May and ended after midday on 16 May in terrible heat. We were still in an enfeebled condition and totally out of training for such a marathon march of thirty-five miles. We had two or three short halts and one of about two hours in the middle of the night. At the end we were totally exhausted and staggered and shuffled in to the outskirts of the village in a daze, scarcely conscious. I really cannot describe the utter exhaustion we felt. As we approached, we could see the village in the distance, amidst the heat haze, but to get our legs to carry us the last two miles seemed an impossible task: but we all, every one, made it in the end, often with the assistance of our friends.

When those of us at the rear straggled in, we were put into a long dark cattle hut with an entrance only at one end and no ventilation. It was dirty, smelly and insufferably hot and airless. We were the last to arrive and were expected to go up to the farthest, darkest and hottest end. Had we settled down there, exhausted as we were, I believe that some of us would have died of heatstroke. There was an Arab guard on the door but I insisted on half the party leaving this death trap and we flung ourselves down in a narrow strip of shade under a mud wall with thankfulness and relief, for here there was a trifling breeze stirring. Some Arabs came along and provided us with water but even then demanded payment for it!

As the heat decreased and the shade extended, we revived remarkably and asked, successfully, for permission to go down to the river below for a most refreshing drink and comprehensive wash. I have never appreciated either more gladly, especially as on this occasion it was free!

Tikrit, already notorious as the birthplace of Saladin, who captured Jerusalem in 1187, gained a very bad reputation in our eyes, the first echelon of prisoners to pass through. Harrowing tales were told to me later by the final echelons of wretched British soldiers relating how some of them had died in misery, sickness and gross neglect or ill-treatment in those very cattle sheds. Years later we heard, without the least regret, that Tikrit had been destroyed by General Maude's army in his historic advance on Mosul in 1917.

On returning that evening to our bivouac area by the sheds we found a number of hawkers of food and fruit ready to do business. Local supplies were plentiful and not expensive and we were now and hereafter expected to arrange for our own messing. I had an enamel washbasin and for our small party we filled it with yoghurt, date treacle and eggs all beaten up together – believe me, a heavenly brew! We consumed large quantities of the nourishing stuff and repeated it next day. Others tried 'leben', sour mare's milk diluted with water, but I never acquired a taste for it.

A special mention must be made of the great green water melons, just the fruit for a parched desert land. Within its thick impervious rind it contains a pinkish-white flesh literally flowing with a thin pleasantly flavoured juice. The very sight of these great green balls, almost the size of a football, gives me a thrill even today. You bought a good slice to eat immediately to quench your thirst. I sympathized with old Jonah at Nineveh (now Mosul) when he showed a display of temper when his gourd withered away. No wonder he ticked off God; I would have done so myself! There is a most graphic description of the incident in the Book of Jonah which I read with enjoyment and sympathy during my six months stay in Mosul.

I have described in detail this first exhausting march to Tikrit in mid-May by a party of officers, mostly young and basically healthy, and with a supply of money, in order that some idea can be formed of the unspeakable sufferings endured by the huge parties of troops which followed in succession after us. Still half-starved, almost without money, some suffering from dysentery, their bones marked the route of the long march of the men of Kut and illustrated their terrible ordeal. From Kut to Baghdad, on again with scarcely a pause, to Mosul and thence to Ras el Ain, 400 miles on foot in the burning heat of summer. Then on again, ever further north across the Toros Mountains into Anatolia, sick, half-naked, driven brutally along, the rascally escort ever ready to steal even their boots if they took them off to ease their aching feet. Unable to keep up with their fellows, they fell out one by one and died in their tracks or were finished off by Arab thieves. If they struggled to some village hut they might be lucky and be taken on by the next column, or might linger on and finally perish in the last extremity of misery and loneliness. Seventy men out of every hundred perished in this way.

For a few, rescue, at least temporarily, was possible. Senior British officers, General Melliss in particular, having transport and money, were able to succour sick and stranded men and carry them forward to the next staging post where they might have a chance of care, if not of survival. In the Toros, much help was given by German personnel working on railway construction projects or on military missions with the Turkish Army, but even so, many died after reaching their final camps.

Although the march to Tikrit was the worst of all, we had at least one more nearly as bad. Much of the blame must rest on the despicable Elmi Bey who was most vague as to the length of the march and as to where water might be found. His calculations were complicated by the fact that, as he apparently knew no Arabic, he could not guess the time that the moon would rise nor how much it might be behind the clouds, the latter point being perhaps excusable.

I cannot explain how it was, but it seemed to happen that my little party often treated the whole trip as a bit of a giggle once we had recovered from the fatigue and exasperation of the moment. At our long midday halts in the burning shade-less desert, Mathais used to rig up a most complicated area of shade with a few selected items from our diminishing kit, a camp bed reared up on end, precariously supported by strings, weights and pegs, eked out with a draping of blankets. It habitually collapsed, causing an outburst of horseplay and hilarity.

There was also in the party a hefty Scottish NCO who stumbled gallantly along, roaring out at intervals, dressed in a mixture of military garments and carrying an old umbrella, with all his r's well rolled:

Blaw the bugle, sound the horn,
Ficht for the Army nicht and morn,
The Hungry Army, tattered and torn,
Back from Abyssinia!

And we came in with the chorus line 'Och! The Hungry Army'.

I think that the ballad may have derived from Napier's campaign in 1868 against King Theodore of Ethiopia and had become traditional.

There was another song very popular later in the camps sung by the infantry and gunner soldiers in Turkey when things were turning out worse than usual:

Wherever we go we always shout
We're buggered if we'll be buggered about,
We won't be buggered about!

I had almost forgotten these capers when I met an elderly Indian clerk in Patna in 1944, nearly thirty years later. He knew my name as I was by then a senior Government official. He asked me if I was the Lieutenant Spackman of the Indian Medical Service on that desert march and, when I acknowledged it, he said:

Sir, I remember you well. You and your friends were always laughing and joking even when things went wrong. I want to tell you that it put heart into us that you could be so light-hearted. It helped us to get through our troubles.

I was much touched by this testimonial and indeed it came as a surprise to me that we had created this impression. I suppose that the old tradition of the grim and often macabre humour of British troops in adversity came to our aid, as it has done throughout our nation's history.

Proceeding on our way north, march after march, we halted a day at Kalat Shargat, the ancient Asshur, with its archaeological excavations initiated by Layard 'of Babylon'. We profited by occupying some of their huts high on the river's bank, the digging having been interrupted by the war. Further north was Hammam Ali, famous for its hot sulphurous springs of which I

100

availed myself ten months later. You could smell the hydrogen sulphur gas a mile off and nearby was an open pool from which crude mineral oil could be skimmed, prophetic of the vast oil fields of present times.

Our dramatic entry into Mosul came on 25 May 1916. When we crested a rise about two miles short of the city, there spread out before us in the distance, were the minarets, domes and substantial stone buildings and houses of this important and prosperous centre. We were formed up into an orderly column by the combined efforts of Elmi (full of self-importance) and our own sense of dignity, and so marched, with something of the old spirit, along what soon became a roughly metalled road lined by well-built villas and gardens. On the south side of a great open space was a massive old caserne which we entered through a deep arched gateway and when inside flung ourselves down, hot, dusty and weary on the paved first-floor gallery facing into the central courtyard. We had marched 170 miles in under ten days and left only one dead man on the way. The columns that followed were not so fortunate.

Chapter Twelve

Left Behind in Mosul, Captive Doctor

Although we had lost only one man on our march to Mosul, several others were seriously ill on arrival there, including two officers, Captain Daniell of the Indian Army and Lieutenant Gregory of the Devonshire Regiment. It was also certain, judging from our experiences in the first echelon, that many more of the parties following us would need hospital care on reaching Mosul, which was only the halfway point on their exhausting march to the railhead at Ras el Ain. The assistance in Mosul of a British doctor might be vitally necessary. I was detailed for the job and remained there for the next six months, the outcome confirming the necessity of such a provision.

Mosul, situated on the right bank of the river, was the first town we had come to which was built largely of stone and baked brick, though supplemented in the poorer quarters by the adobe mud walls found in tropical towns and villages throughout the world. All the houses had the usual flat roofs, sometimes with little penthouses on them, on which the inmates slept at night during hot weather.

At the upper end of the town a short bridge of boats led to a fine stone viaduct carrying the road to Kurdistan and Persia (now Iran). On the left bank at this point were great bare mounds extending for miles, marking the site of Nineveh, that wicked city inveigled against by the prophet Jonah. On one smaller, steeper mound was a small mosque revered as the tomb of Jonah by Jews, Moslems and Christians alike; one of the largest is said to mark the site of the Palace of King Sennacherib.

It was excavated in 1840 by the archaeologist, Layard.

After two days' rest in the noisy caserne, the rest of the first echelon was sent forward on its long trek to Ras el Ain. I and my patients felt very forlorn after saying goodbye to our special friends and comrades almost none of whom, had we known it, we were ever to see again. The two officers left behind were very ill with dysentery and half a dozen other ranks were quite unfit to proceed owing to the same complaint or to ulcerated sores on their feet. Luckily I had kept well, having inherited a good constitution and a sound pair of legs.

The Turkish officer in charge of the barracks, which was also a staging post on the Turkish lines of communication, was the 'Merkez Commandani', Bimbashi (Major) Umar Bey. Like so many of the officials we were unfortunate to serve under while 'guests' of the Turks, he was an idle and elusive person who only attended to official business in a most easy going and dilatory fashion for a short time every morning, while drinking his morning cups of strong black coffee. He might turn up in the evenings if he felt like it, to have a chat or because some important functionary was passing through Mosul. In practice, there were many mornings when he never turned up at all and then everything came to a dead stop.

My difficulties were much increased because none of the Turks could speak English. To get over this handicap, I tried to recollect some French, that admirable language so widely understood, if not spoken, throughout the Middle East. In the absence of language primers or serious books, I was assisted by being able to borrow some rather salty French novels and some old copies of *La Vie Parisienne*. Later, a decent little Jew called Selim was engaged as interpreter and I got him to give me systematic instruction in Turkish, not a difficult language as the grammar is regular and the construction logical. In later months my Turkish, elementary but conversationally fluent, proved to be of great assistance to me and to others and helped solve many problems.

How long we would have been left camped on the bare and dirty boards of that caserne I do not know but, by good fortune, on the day following the departure of my friends, the War Minister, the all-powerful Enver Pasha, came to Mosul on inspection and, when he visited the barracks, he asked for me to go and see him.

It was astonishing what a change came over the scene in the presence of this personage. A new and electric atmosphere seemed to affect everyone, much tinged with apprehension. Rather short but powerfully built, with the look of a determined and ruthless man, favouring upturned moustaches in the Prussian manner and wearing an impeccably cut uniform with many decorations, including the Iron Cross (he had spent time in Germany studying their methods and ideas), he was accompanied by a group of well turned out young officers.

He was reputed to have built up his powerful position and achieved his aims by free use of terrorist methods, including having shot, with his own revolver, several men who stood in his way during his ascent to power. During the time of the Balkan Wars, in company with Tala'at and Djemal, he had founded the Young Turk Party and the Committee of Union and Progress . In 1913, at the end of one phase of these wars, Enver Pasha burst into a Cabinet meeting in Constantinople (now Istanbul) and shot dead the then Minister of War, Nazim Pasha, who was about to conclude a Peace Treaty which Enver considered to be very unfavourable to Turkish interests. He had then consolidated his position with the old regime by marrying the Sultan's daughter. Quite a success story!

It must be added, however, that he had to flee his homeland at the end of the First World War when Turkey was defeated. Of his subsequent adventures and intrigues with and against the Bolsheviks in the Emirates of Central Asia and of the peculiar circumstances attending his violent death, very little is known. He is said to have been beheaded by Cossacks in a wild valley in Turkestan, a fate clearly in accord with the vicissitudes of his turbulent life but, in fact, it is doubtful if it really was Enver who had been killed in that summer of 1922. In his book *A Person from England*, Sir Fitzroy Maclean has been able to throw some light on these final chapters in the life of one of the most colourful persons of that time. But that is another story and we must return to Mosul.

Enver was in Umar Bey's office at the entrance to the barracks when I was shown in. He offered me his hand, without a gun in it, and asked me through an interpreter if I was satisfactorily accommodated. I replied at once that my two sick officers and three others ought to be in hospital and that their present billet, the bare boards of a barrack block, were quite unsuitable for them. Enver turned angrily to the senior Turkish doctor, who became pale and incoherent with alarm, and ordered that my request be carried out at once.

The hospital, though primitive, was a great improvement on the barracks. I had a pleasant room, like a penthouse, on the upper floor. My sick personnel were given beds in the wards and I was able to look after them within the limited means at my disposal. An Indian subordinate doctor named Manikam was allowed to remain for a few weeks to help me at a time when many fresh sick began to arrive. To cope with the nursing there were four Greek or Armenian nuns and a few untrained nursing orderlies. The British and Indian sick, arriving with the marching columns, gradually took over nearly all the beds.

Poor little Gregory, very ill and homesick, was my chief care and Daniell, sick as he was, helped me to attend to him but it was sad work and medically unrewarding. The poor lad died of acute choleric dysentery within three days of moving to the hospital. We had only been installed in the hospital a day or so when parties of officers and men began to come into the barracks close by, arriving in the early morning without advance news that they were expected. In order to facilitate my work I had given my captors a sort of limited and local parole which permitted me to go freely across to both the barracks and to a small restaurant on the other side of the main square. If I wanted to go into town I had to take a guard (a 'posta') and usually Selim as interpreter.

I made it a routine practice to go across to Umar Bey's office every morning after my ward round. If he was there, he would be sitting cross-legged on a carpet covered wooden settee behind his desk, at his ease with tunic unbuttoned and military cap beside him, his scruffy hair uncovered. A cup of black Turkish coffee would be on the desk before him, with a long handled pot to replenish it, beside a dish of reed pens with a sifter of sand to dry the ink on his letters. After making the regulation gestures of salutation and then taking a seat on a bug-ridden chair, I would, after a suitable period of silence, enquire if there was any news, a purely formal question always answered in the negative. A long pause would follow. His mind, when it was functioning, worked very slowly. I would then be offered a cup of coffee or perhaps a cigarette, for he was essentially an amiable old bird, though bone idle.

I might then ask if any fresh prisoners of war had arrived and he would send out to enquire. It was not allowed for me to go up and see for myself but fortunately there was a Turkish military doctor attached to the barracks and together we inspected the new arrivals, sending over to the hospital any that required more than simple treatment. Almost daily I had some request or protest to register with the Commandant but I soon learnt that it was useless to storm in about it. I could usually get what I wanted by observing the oriental formalities.

On one occasion, a very gallant and senior British General was so filled with indignation and wrath by what he had seen of the plight of our poor troops marching up from Samarra that he rushed into Umar Bey's office and, thumping the table, demanded in a loud and peremptory voice that transport and assistance be sent off immediately to bring them along. Although the matter was, in truth, most urgent, the result was entirely negative, an evasive reply being a Turkish speciality; the matter was not within local competence and must be referred to Constantinople (what a hope!); 'yaren' (tomorrow, meaning a vague and improbable future); 'olojek' (equally vague, 'it will be done'). You rarely got a frank 'yok, effendi' (no, Sir). My own trump card, but one which I kept up my sleeve for the most exceptional crises, was to introduce Enver's name, saying he had promised me so and so.

In the hospital things did not prosper. I can hardly bear to think of that hospital even now. Diet was monotonous and restricted. The chief items were yoghurt and rather sour wheaten bread, both healthy items but disliked by my poor patients who tried to buy less suitable stuff at the hospital gate. For me it was a daily penance going on my ward round, for it was easy to tell which patients were suffering from the terrible and apparently incurable wasting dysentery, a condition that one seemed to be able to smell in their breath. They would linger on for weeks, getting thinner and more wasted until they invariably died. They saw their pals drop off one by one till their own turn came and it was impossible to give them any hope that rang with conviction. Sadly I watched Captain Daniell fall into this state and it was agony to know that he realized that, despite having a tremendous will to live, he had no chance though he lasted several weeks. [editor's note: Captain Hubert J. Daniell was the elder son of Major General J.F. Daniell, CMG, GOC Sierra Leone. Born 1888 he passed out first at Sandhurst, gaining the King's medal. Gazetted to the Indian Infantry, after attachment to General Delamain's staff, he served in the siege of Kut, gaining a Mention in Dispatches.]

I lost nearly 100 British soldiers in that melancholy hospital in a period of a few weeks that summer. I had them all buried by a local priest of the Greek Orthodox Church at a place called the Hote el Americain, a bare hillside two miles south-west of Mosul and I put up two memorial stones and filled in the official 'acte de deces' for each man. After the war this cemetery was found with its marking stones by the British War Graves Commission who had it properly fenced in and arranged for its maintenance.

There was a considerable difference in the conduct and appearance of the British and Indian units as they came through Mosul and it was not always to the credit of the British. It was hardly to be expected that much discipline and organization could survive the hardships of those marches and the privations which the men suffered. Also, I formed the opinion that the Turks, for political reasons, treated the Indians with more consideration than the British. I must, however, record that whereas, regrettably, many units of both races arrived in Mosul more like a ragged rabble, each man fending for himself or with a single companion to share with, two or three Indian units, e.g.

the 2/7th Gurkhas and the 48th Pioneers, marched in gallantly in company formation under their Havildars. Moreover my dear 48th Pioneers actually came to me with a sum of money with which they asked me to buy them raisins and flour which they took on with them for use on the onward march.

I considered it my duty to try to encourage self-respect and soldierly behaviour amongst the men during their short stay in Mosul, as well as to weed out such men as were unfit to march. Some of the British were half-naked and had only rags or old puttees bound on their feet, having foolishly parted with their tunics and boots to buy food, or having had these articles stolen. I had to argue constantly with my Turkish 'colleague' as to who was fit to go forward and who should stay for rest or treatment. He was always anxious to push them along and out of his sphere of responsibility, a typical Turkish attitude.

One lot of men had a particularly poor record of bad conduct, quarrelling and fighting amongst themselves. One man was reported to me by his sergeant for selling a fellow soldier's boots, which he had stolen just after they reached Mosul. I paraded the men and pointed out that under the prevailing circumstances and the fact that they were due to go forward to Ras el Ain next day, such an act was tantamount to murdering his colleague. There were other complaints against this man who evidently was a thoroughly bad hat. I felt that an example must be made of him. I therefore asked the Turks to try him and administer a public punishment without delay. As a result he was bastinadoed, beaten on the bare soles of his feet, a singularly appropriate punishment, in front of the others in his party and in my presence. Actually in this case it was not carried out with much vigour but it had a good moral effect. I had to keep him back for a few days but he took his punishment philosophically, so far as I could tell.

I had by this time obtained a small fund from the International Red Cross and with this I was able to provide those in need with a certain number of shoes or sandals as well as additional food. I managed to borrow from the Turks a large copper cooking pot and arranged for a meat and vegetable stew to be prepared daily to supplement the poor quality Turkish ration. I tried to get only mutton or goat but sometimes only beef was obtainable. When Indians asked me what was in the stew I always said I didn't know but that all who liked could have a helping. It always smelt extremely tempting to the hungry men and one sniff was usually enough to overcome any religious doubts or caste prejudices which they held.

The maximum number staging in Mosul at one stage reached 4,000 men but soon dwindled down to 100 or so, including those in the hospital. The Turks had a desire to put on parade a virile British Division which had been defeated by their valiant army, for the delight of the local population and the much needed restoration of the morale of their own army. This was never achieved. No body of surrendering troops can be expected to show much military glitter and display and even after the weeding out of so many debilitated men, both in Kut and later in Baghdad, there remained nothing of military might for the Turks to gloat over.

One morning, on returning to the hospital, I was told that my cousin had called to see me. By this time I had learnt to be surprised at nothing but even so was hardly prepared to be embraced by a robust English lady! However I played my part in the presence of the inevitable Turkish official and we exchanged enquiries about a few fictitious friends and relatives. It appeared that a small party of British subjects employed in Baghdad had been interned and were being sent by easy stages to Constantinople.

They were quartered in a house nearby, protected by a small guard and they kindly invited me to lunch with them next day. One of their husbands had been a bank manager, one a river pilot and one an irrigation engineer, whose wife, Mrs Whitley, had with her a delightful small daughter, Daphne, aged about three, to whom I immediately lost my heart. Daphne lived near us in England after the Second World War.

These good ladies expressed the desire to help the troops, so I set them the task of making up little bags of raisins, which were plentiful and cheap, one bag for each man as an emergency ration, and gave them money for this purpose. I learnt afterwards that the kind ladies had returned the money by enclosing a small silver coin in each bag.

I also received unexpected help from a friendly Austrian Warrant Officer named Schlosser who was in Mosul for a few days buying horses for the Austrian Transport Mission. I had struck up an acquaintance with him at the restaurant by the barracks. He told me he formerly worked in Jaffa in an orange exporting business which had close friendly relations with a British firm there. He said he had a fund of Turkish gold pounds as well as paper currency with which to buy horses and he promised me in strict confidence that he would give me gold for paper currency if I could bring him the latter next day. The matter being very secret as well as urgent as he was leaving at noon next day, I was only able to raise about twenty-five pounds in notes in the time available but, as gold was worth about four times paper, the transaction was most rewarding. Whether it was strictly ethical behaviour on his part was no concern of mine; at least it was entirely altruistic!

I concluded another financial deal in Mosul soon after, this time concerning roubles. A number of Russians captured on the Persian front were in the barracks for a couple of days and one of them spoke French. He asked me to change their rouble notes for Turkish currency. I was able to get quite a good rate from a Persian acquaintance who, mistakenly, trusted the stability of the Russian rouble against the Turkish pound. Within six months the Bolshevik Revolution had broken out in Moscow and the rouble notes were worthless!

The restaurant at which I was allowed to take two meals a day was situated on the far side of a big open square in front of the barracks. It was run by a merry, fat little one-eyed Italian named Enrico, otherwise Henriques in deference to his handsome French wife who, like a good Frenchwoman, supervised the cooking and catering very competently, while he looked after the business side, which included keeping certain Turkish officials in good humour. The name of this place was the Stamboul Locanta and, as it was the only place serving European style food, as opposed to the many small Arab eating houses, it had a monopoly in its own field. Enrico and his wife

110

had several bilingual children of whom the youngest boy was a special favourite of mine. He had a charming way of mixing French and Italian in his chatter. One day this poor child fell ill with acute appendicitis. There followed two dreadful days of anxiety. I was not allowed to operate, and indeed had no facilities to do so, nor could I get real help from the Turkish doctor, and so this little boy's life was lost from peritonitis and septicaemia.

Enrico must have made a handsome profit during the time all the Kut officers were streaming through Mosul on their way north, though his charges seemed reasonable. He showed his confidence in our honesty by letting anyone have credit or be allowed to pay by cheques drawn on his own notepaper. As our officers were being sent off in batches at short notice it says a lot for our honesty that when all the officers had gone through I offered to settle any outstanding accounts out of consular funds; he told me that the figure was so insignificant that he would not ask for it.

The prosperity of the Stamboul Restaurant excited the cupidity of a certain Tahsin Effendi, a pharmacist (erzachi) who was much addicted to raki and often drunk, an incompetent worthless individual who was some sort of relation to Umar Bey. He persuaded the local civil administrator that it was wrong for a Franco-Italian family to be even temporarily in a position to meet British prisoners and, using these arguments, he succeeded after a time in ousting Enrico and taking over the restaurant himself. The restaurant was also used for meals by some better class Turks and by any German officers passing through. Such was Tahsin's gross incompetence that its reputation fell to zero. This allowed Enrico to regain control, this time with the help of a bright young Arab named Yusep, by moving to the premises of the former Officers' Club on the river bank. Yusep was a lively character who wore a particularly bright scarlet fez and had (or rather we accredited to him) a dashing reputation with regard to the local girls. He had a roguish eye and liked to be credited with a reputation for gallantry.

Although I was once ordered out of the restaurant by a swaggering young Prussian officer who professed to be insulted by my very presence while he ate, I got on well with the usual patrons. On one occasion when I was lunching there, a party of Arab officers came in and cheerfully ordered a round of drinks. It happened to be the end of the month of Ramadan and the new moon had just been seen, an occasion for rejoicing at the end of a great month of fasting. They were all in a most festive mood, having evidently started the celebrations elsewhere, and called out seasonal greetings to me, to which I responded as best I could. One of them then sent over to me a good big tot of raki. We drank each other's health with great enthusiasm on their side. Unfortunately, this idea spread and each one in turn decided to honour me. I managed to swallow four of these potent tots in quick succession but when the fifth arrived I decided that enough was enough but did not like to refuse the compliment. Luckily I was sitting with my back to a large potted palm and, taking advantage of their careless rapture, I managed with a bit of sleight of hand, to toss the libation into it, quickly bringing the empty glass to my lips with every appearance of enjoyment. They were so impressed with my prowess in drinking that I had some difficulty in breaking away from their boisterous company!

Having so little to do, I used to linger over my meals at a table outside the restaurant watching the scenes and movements on the great square. Passing through I might see a group of travel stained Turkish soldiers in their faded green uniforms, or a haughty German strutting past in his jackboots. So as not to be outdone, I commissioned the local boot maker to make me a similar pair in soft Russian leather and then walked about just as proudly. But the sight which pleased me most was to see the splendid Kurds with their wide trousers of home-woven colours, boat-shaped shoes with red pompoms, short jackets and voluminous waist scarves stuffed full of daggers and pistols who full well knew the admiration they inspired. Proud independent tribesmen, living in their villages high in the remote and inaccessible mountains of Kurdistan, they only nominally acknowledge the authority of the Turkish Government which did not attempt to bring them under full civil control. They despised the Arabs of the flat plains of

Lieutenant W.C. Spackman,
Indian Medical Service, at
home, Christmas 1913.
Author

The Spackman
brothers, L to R, Eric,
Charles, Bill, Maurice.
Author

Ashar Creek, Basra, November 1914. *By kind permission of the Imperial War Museum. Ref: Q92163*

HMS *Lawrence* at Qurna, December 1914. *By kind permission of the Imperial War Museum. Ref: Q92674*

A boat from HMS *Espiegle* used to cross a deep creek, Qurna, January 1915. *By kind permission of the Imperial War Museum. Ref: Q92178*

British and Indian troops near Qurna. *By kind permission of the Imperial War Museum. Ref: Q92676*

British trenches at Qurna, January 1915. *By kind permission of the Imperial War Museum. Ref: Q92677*

River steamer *Mejidieh* with 18-pounder gun on top deck. *By kind permission of the Imperial War Museum. Ref: Q92638*

48th Pioneers embarking on the captured Turkish steamer *Mejidieh*, 1915. *By kind permission of the Imperial War Museum. Ref: Q92679*

120th Rajputana Infantry covering the retirement from the village of Alloa, January 1915. *By kind permission of the National Army Museum. Ref: 94554*

48th Pioneers crossing flooded land near Shaiba, April 1915. *By kind permission of the Imperial War Museum. Ref: Q92684*

Officers of the 48th Pioneers halt for a meal. *By kind permission of the Imperial War Museum. Ref: Q92691*

Sheik of Zobeir and Colonel Smith at Abu, 1915. *By kind permission of the Imperial War Museum. Ref: Q92683*

Moving troops by bellum (native boats). *By kind permission of the National Army Museum. Ref: 94555*

A British advanced Brigade HQ at a captured Turkish trench. *By kind permission of the Imperial War Museum. Ref: Q24407*

A hospital launch *H5* on the River Tigris. *By kind permission of the Imperial War Museum. Ref: Q15252*

A captured 5.9-inch Howitzer. *By kind permission of Central Press/Getty Images. Ref: CP224-5*

The Arch of Ctesiphon. The battle around it was from 22-24 November 1915. *By kind permission of the Imperial War Museum. Ref: Q24446*

3 yoke of bullocks pulling a spare 18-pounder gun during the retreat from Ctesiphon. *By kind permission of the Imperial War Museum. Ref: Q92654*

Major General Townshend at his quarters at Kut during the siege. *By kind permission of the Imperial War Museum. Ref: Q70247*

13-pounder field gun mounted in the defences of Kut for firing at enemy aircraft, 1916. *By kind permission of the Imperial War Museum. Ref: Q92663*

Army surgeons operate in a makeshift theatre open to the skies during the siege. *By kind permission of the Imperial War Museum. Ref: Q92665*

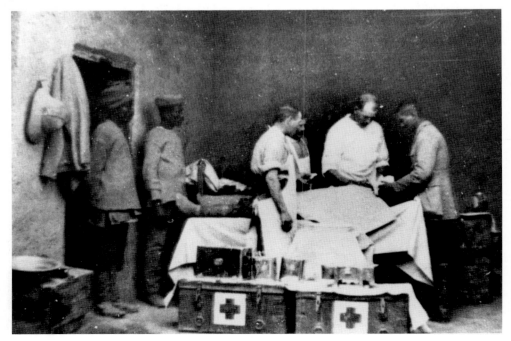

Destroying an 18-pounder gun before surrender April 1916. *By kind permission of the Imperial War Museum. Ref: Q106226*

With the British in Mesopotamia, a river gunboat. *By kind permission of Central Press/Getty Images. Ref: CP224-6*

A British artillery observation post in the desert near Kut, Relief Force. *By kind permission of the Imperial War Museum. Ref: Q24410*

The Relief Force Wireless Station receiving possibly the last message from Kut. *By kind permission of the National Army Museum. Ref: 94432*

British artillery limbers captured after destruction at Kut. *By kind permission of the National Army Museum. Ref: 94563*

The Fall of Kut. General Townsend and his captors, 29 April 1916. *By kind permission of the Imperial War Museum. Ref: Q79344*

An emaciated, surviving Indian soldier after the siege. *By kind permission of the Imperial War Museum. Ref: Q79446*

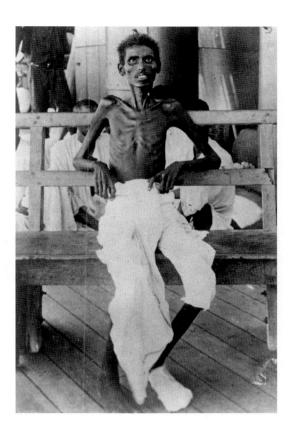

Turkish soldiers and baggage travelling on a recently opened light railway, April 1917. *By kind permission of the Imperial War Museum. Ref: Q57203*

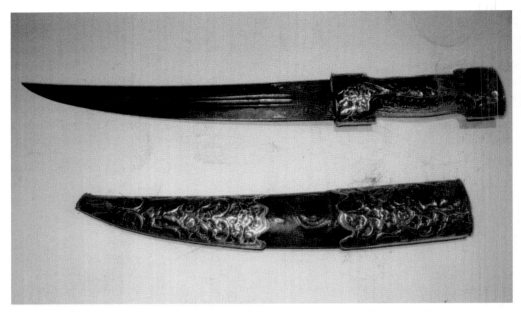

The Persian dagger presented to Captain Spackman, inscribed 'Allah is Merciful'. *Author*

A contemporary German representation of the British surrender at Kut, April 1916. *By kind permission of the National Army Museum*

Mesopotamia and are, even now, in constant revolt against the present rulers of Iraq. I have much sympathy for them.

I was walking one day from the hospital to the Stamboul Locanta when I was surprised to see in the middle of the square a body hanging from a gallows. Public hangings were sometimes carried out for civil offences. The technique was to stand the culprit on a table with his hands tied behind his back and a noose around his neck. The table would then be pulled away. He would swing and give a brief wriggle but lost consciousness almost at once due to the rope cutting off the blood supply to his brain. Though unconscious he would actually be alive for many minutes.

This particular hanging well illustrated the rough and ready wartime methods of local justice then practised. It appears that a murder had been committed and the relations of the murderer got hold of some half-witted person and persuaded him to confess to the crime on the pretext that they would then square the judge and get the accused acquitted, after which they would handsomely reward him. Unfortunately the judicial authorities took the easy way out by stringing him up without delay! My informant regarded the matter as rather a good joke!

Another gruesome sight took place almost weekly on the river bank below the hospital and in full view of my window. This was the place for public executions by shooting. The Turks were ruthless in their dealings with the various tribes under their domination. Individuals convicted or even suspected of spying or desertion were brought here in batches to be shot. It was all done very openly and a crowd of spectators accompanied the troop of soldiers escorting the victims as they were taken out of the local jail and down to the river bank.

Here the reprobates were lined up against the cliff and blind-folded, then arranged at three yard intervals, each having opposite him four riflemen under an NCO. The signal to fire was given by an officer dropping a white flag which was seen by the NCOs, reminiscent of the start of a horse race. By dint of frequent practice, the result was technically pretty good although occasionally the officer had to take his revolver to finish off some poor wretch squirming on the ground.

113

When the river level fell in early autumn, better use was made of the long stretches of exposed river bed by sowing and raising crops of maize and water melon. Because all the town sewage drifted down onto this area, this created a fertile field.

I was able to write home from Mosul after an interval, counting the siege, of eight months but I had to be strictly factual being limited to only four lines on an official postcard. I have some of these postcards beside me, with deletions made by the censor in Constantinople and stamped by the Red Crescent and the Red Cross who transmitted them. They took eight weeks to reach England but relieved my family of anxiety. One I signed as from Lieutenant Spackman but in the next, a few days later, I signed as a Captain. By my service timescale, I knew I was due this promotion and on my telling Umar Bey he obligingly accepted it and thereafter I drew an extra one pound a month! Through the kindness of a German Army doctor, I also sent one quite long letter through the 'Feldpost, der Deutschen Militär mission' on the occasion that they inoculated me against cholera and typhoid. This letter got home in good time but my subsequent moves prevented me from hearing anything from home for a further period of nine months, making a total of nearly two years without news of my three brothers and one sister, all on war service, or of my elderly parents. All survived to meet up with me again after the war.

There was no such thing as a reliable public clock in these isolated eastern towns and no one bothered much about exact punctuality. The sun was usually visible at sunset and this fixed the daily time, proclaimed by the muezzins from the minarets. This was the famous Desert Time we all observed where sunset was always twelve o'clock, rather confusing at first and needing some calculation. If you wished to meet someone at one o'clock it meant one hour after sunset, and so on. Of course you had to keep altering your watch as the seasons changed. A similar convention prevailed in Venice in Casanova's time, except for sunset being twenty-four o'clock, quite a modern touch.

A further complication arose over the question of date. The Turks were keeping the old Orthodox calendar, with a difference of thirteen days from ours. This made it difficult filling in the death reports in my hospital returns so I put in both

114

dates and hoped for the best. Later the Turks reformed their calendar under pressure from their German allies, despite considerable religious opposition.

Important people were constantly passing through Mosul, usually to or from Persia or Baghdad. One such I met was Sven Hedin, the famous Swedish explorer who was touring the war fronts as a 'neutral' war correspondent but, in fact, promoting strong German propaganda. He saw fit to treat me in a brusque and unfriendly way. I disliked him intensely.

One day when I was taking a meal at Enrico's, almost certainly tomato omelette, stewed apricots and yoghurt, with bread and sour cream, I noticed at a corner table a small party of officers wearing a rather distinctive uniform, neither Turkish nor German. I had plenty of time, being in no hurry to re-enter the sizzling heat of June, nor were the waiters or fat Arab cook attentive, so I had time to study the group. The principal figure was a handsome man of middle age, well shaved and with carefully clipped moustache and well-tended hands. He was accompanied by a Turkish Captain I came to know later as Ahmed Bey and by two young officers of his own race. I had just decided that it was time to make the effort of walking the half mile back to the hospital in order to escape the flies and cooking smells, intending on the way to buy a slice of water melon to eat with Madame Enrico's ginger biscuits for my tea after my siesta, when one of the officers came across and asked me in French if I would join 'his Excellency' for coffee and a Greek liqueur. Being bored with my own company, I gladly took up my little palm leaf fan and went across to be introduced. I gathered that his name was Kyril (he wrote it down for me in Russian characters on the back of a greasy menu) and that he was a Prince of Georgia who had been exiled by the Russian Government. His present appointment was that of Colonel of a Caucasian Brigade which he had raised to fight against the Russians on the Persian front where his troops were already engaged. He was expecting to join them 'in a few days' but was awaiting Turkish permission to do so.

In response to his invitation I visited his tents two days later, accompanied by my Turkish posta and interpreter Selim. We crossed the river by the bridge of boats and the stone viaduct to where the caravan route starts that winds up through the hills to El Khoosh and its extremely ancient monastery inhabited by Chaldean monks. The Chaldeans were a peaceful and submissive people who thus escaped the massacres which befell their neighbours the Armenians. Another road led south-east to the still undeveloped town of Kirkuk, blissfully unaware of its future in the oil producing world.

Kyril was temporarily out so Selim took me up the steep mound on which stood the tomb of Jonah and I was accorded the unusual privilege of entering the little mosque after first removing my shoes. There was little to see inside so I asked the mullah if there were any relics of Jonah. He pointed to two jaws of sword fish, of quite unusual size, hanging on the wall and assured me that they were the jaws of the famous whale!

We walked about on the great mound where Senacherib's Palace had stood, with the deep excavations made by the archaeologists still visible, and looked out over the desolation of mounds; all that was left of the famous city of Nineveh. I wondered if in 2,000 years London might look like that.

On returning we found that Kyril was back at his tents on the grassy bank by the river and we admired his fine horses tethered there. I had smartened up my appearance so far as I was able and was wearing my new top boots for the occasion.

Kyril took me inside his tent, which contained a minimum of furniture. On the camp table was a worn volume of Victor Hugo's poems and a couple of Yuruk saddlebags containing other books and personal clothing. The inventory was completed by a camp bed, toilet stand, two yakdans which could be carried on pack animals which were beside the entrance and some saddlery. He offered me some melon and then coffee was brought in. Our conversation, assisted by Selim, was carried on in French and was somewhat limited by the fact that neither of us was fluent in that language. Nevertheless, I gathered that in the days before the Russo-Japanese War he had lived in a castle in the mountains of Georgia but had then quarrelled with the Russian Government and had been banished after taking part in an open revolt, escaping by boat in

116

a hasty crossing of the Black Sea to Trebizond in Turkey and thence travelling to safety in a residence in Lausanne.

At the outbreak of the 1914-1918 War he returned to Turkey with the aim of fighting against Russia, leading a band of his followers on the Caucasian Front. To date, local Turkish jealousy had prevented him getting further than Mosul, though the bulk of his contingent had gone forward while he waited to get permission to join them. I knew only too well how easily the Turks could delay his obtaining this permit by employing methods with which I was familiar. Almost every time I met him that summer he told me he was about to leave!

The Prince did not seem to feel the heat much himself. In the middle of a July afternoon he would send for me with a hired barouche asking me to see one of his entourage who was sick. By then he had moved into a house near the serai for the sake of his staff and horses and would confound me with a large veterinary thermometer, graduated in centigrade, (and a reamur) with which he took everyone's temperature. When I came to see one of his servants who had malaria without bringing my stethoscope, he was so put out that he sent a man to fetch it.

Finally, one August evening, as I was crossing the square to ask Madame Enriques to make me some more ginger biscuits, I saw a barouche turn sharply in my direction. Out jumped the Prince and with extended hand he cried 'Pray congratulate me Monsieur le Docteur, I am off to the war at last!' I gravely offered my congratulations with as fresh and sincere a manner as I could manage and asked for further details. Yes, he had seen Haidar Bey, the Vali, and got his papers signed and his transport was at the caserne entrance waiting to start. I accompanied him as he went to say goodbye to Umar Bey after which he gave me a parting gift of a copy of a *Life of Napoleon* by Bourienne and a novel by Zola. Bearing these I returned to Enrico's and mentioned to him that Kyril seemed to be off at last. Enrico snatched his hat and hurried out exclaiming ' Mon Dieu, he owes me 2,000 piastres!'

During the following weeks there were reports of heavy fighting in the mountains beyond Ravandoos but no word of the

Prince. Then, on a day in late October, I met Ahmed Bey, his Turkish staff officer. 'Ah M. le Docteur, His Excellency has been enquiring for you. He is in the Club garden, come over and see him.' Over coffee and the usual sugary liqueur I asked him his news.

Yes, there had been much fighting and he and his men had killed many Russians. But fever had broken out and he himself had had much sickness, had been invalided out and was returning to Constantinople from where he would probably retire to Lausanne and take no further part in the war. He would not be returning to Georgia as he was not sympathetic to the Bolsheviks.

I learnt later that he had had constant rows and become involved in petty jealousies with the Turkish command at Ravandoos but that as a result of his Christian followers having been seen to be less ruthless in dealing with the local population than the Moslem Turks, he had been relieved of his command and sent back 'with a flea in his ear'! This picturesque and temperamental aristocrat did, I hope, find Lausanne a peaceful retreat thereafter.

Returning to my daily life, in the early autumn work in the hospital diminished. Poor Daniell grew thinner, weaker and died. My soldiers either died or got better and the latter were then sent off to camps in the north. I had more time on my hands and began to become bored. I took to playing 'towlu', backgammon, with the Turks and Arabs on the little tables outside the local coffee shop, a game I had not played since childhood, an amusing game requiring a skilful mixture of caution and risk-taking, a very ancient game still played for high stakes at a famous London club. In the east they played it at great speed, using a curious mixture of Turkish, Persian and Arabic. If the dice were both fours it was 'dort', Turkish, 'jahar', Persian, and similar mixtures, whilst if you specially wanted some number but missed it you cursed the dice 'Ta! Edebsiz kemek!' (Yah, shameless bone.)

The evenings were very pleasant in the Officers' Club garden on the banks of the Tigris. I had two friends who dined with me there, a delightful little Carmelite monk called Pere Albert and a

Baghdad Jew, Ephraim Toeg, whose business was to buy wool. It was the season of the year when fruit was plentiful and we often finished our meal by picking grapes from a huge bunch hanging out in the open air. Sometimes there were large thin skinned yellow figs fresh from the Kurdistan hills to the east, the most delicious I have ever tasted.

For exercise I used to swim. Walking as an exercise was considered senseless and also involved taking a posta with me. The only clean place to enter the water and come out was at some steps in the Club garden. I used to swim upstream in the slack water till driven out by a projecting wall, then dash out at my best speed into the swift current and try to reach a half-submerged old brick arch in mid-stream before being swept past it. I usually failed.

It began to be a dull, lonely life and I longed for a change.

Chapter Thirteen

Journey in Hope

To travel hopefully is a better thing than to arrive.

R.L. Stevenson

Early in November 1916 I saw my last two soldier patients leave hospital for their long desert journey en route for the prisoner of war camps in Anatolia. They were in as good physical condition as could be expected and were glad to be on their way. I had been able to get them a lift as far as Ras el Ain on an Austrian motor lorry so that they would not have to undertake the terrible march which had destroyed so many of their fellows travelling in the earlier, larger groups.

I had feared that I might automatically be sent off with them but there seemed to be some uncertainty about my disposal. As usual, I could get no clue about my future from the Merkez Commandi though I kept pleading that the all powerful Enver Pasha had said that I, as a doctor, could be repatriated when my work was done. Actually no such promise had been given but it was well known that I had had an interview with him in May and, as Enver's name was a password past many minor officials, I had taken a suitable opportunity, when there were several people present in Umar Bey's office taking coffee, to mention this 'fact'!

I did not have many days to wait for just then Khalil Pasha, the Army Commander on the Tigris front, made one of his occasional visits to Mosul and I obtained an interview with him. I spun the same story about Enver, who was his father-in-law, and reminded him that a number of British doctors captured at

Kut al Amara, who had got no further north than Baghdad, had been transferred across the Tigris frontline when their services were no longer required. After all, my request for repatriation was a reasonable one but I could scarcely conceal my relief and joy when he not only agreed to my request, but then actually initialled an order for my dispatch down the river to Baghdad as a first step. At that time General Maude's army below Kut, facing the same old Turkish positions at Sannaiyat, was practically static and my transfer across to British lines between the two armies should present no serious problem, though I expected to be most interested in the method of transfer, not to mention its outcome!

I was thrilled in anticipation of spending Christmas 1916 on the right side of the lines. Little did I dream that five months later I would march wearily back into Mosul with no more kit than I could carry slung over my shoulder in my old sleeping bag, though still able to laugh cynically at my own misfortunes?

Oblivious of this reverse waiting in store for me, I felt on top of the world. My health was fully restored and thanks to the necessity of eating quantities of yoghurt I had got rid of the nagging chronic dysentery that had worried me ever since the siege. Furthermore I rarely felt the effects of the touch of malaria which I had in Amara the previous summer. My physical condition and spirits were at a peak and my age was 26.

I was not worried about my journey down to Baghdad, as I knew that the Turks would not repatriate me with a bad send-off. I expected to travel by araba, a four-wheeled covered cart, the height of luxury though spring less and bug-ridden, but to my great joy I was granted the unique experience of a voyage right down the Tigris to Baghdad on a kelek. My preparations for leaving were quickly completed and the local parole I had given (necessary for the efficient performance of my duties in aid of our prisoners passing through Mosul) was cancelled.

These keleks were rafts of a construction going back to the time of Cyrus and are described by Xenophon in his Anabasis. They consisted of a platform of poplar poles bound together and cross-woven with withy twigs and branches to give a roughly level surface with an extra ledge for a sleeping couch.

Underneath and to give buoyancy were goat skins inflated with air. They carried quite a lot of cargo, which had to be stowed so as to keep the craft on an even balance and in such a way as to avoid the cargo falling off into the water from any sudden jolt, such as from touching a sandbank while rounding a bend.

Economically, the scheme was a sound one. On arrival, the rafts were dismantled; the poles were sold in Baghdad for building purposes and the deflated skins taken back by donkey over the desert.

The great day of departure arrived and I went down to the river bank where the keleks were constructed, accompanied or seen off by almost all my varied collection of friends. Even lazy old Umar Bey left his official seat in the barracks entrance to see me off. Mine was the only kelek leaving that day. It was about twelve feet square and had a nice little bower where, on a pile of leafy twigs, I made a bed out of my kilim, carpets and an old sleeping bag. I had two Turkish soldiers to guard me, more for protection en route than to prevent me from trying to escape, which was the last thing I would have attempted to do under the circumstances! As crew there were two kelekchis to guide the kelek down river with their poles. It was a bit crowded with room taken up by our official baggage plus a 'bit on the side' for trading purposes belonging to the kelekchis, but why worry?

When anyone departed it was the pleasant custom for his friends to bring presents for his journey and soon my raft was well stocked with fresh, fragrant and pliable wafer cake, figs, grapes, eggs, local cheese, lettuce and melons. There were also some sausages, hard as wood. These I recognized, for I had seen them hanging in a shop, old and too mummified even to attract flies! Much more acceptable, and most surprising, was a present of half-a dozen bottles of Guinness stout. I cannot remember if it was still drinkable, probably not, or whether I gave them to the crew. I had a small supply of raki, carefully hidden, which was invaluable to disguise the taste of the river water as well as for its other more pleasant properties.

After cordial greetings and lengthy farewells, I clambered aboard and we cast off, waving to our assembled friends, setting out into the sparkling waters of the river. We drifted downstream, past the ancient brickwork arch in mid-stream that I had so often failed to reach in my evening swims, past the hospital and my vacant room on the roof overlooking the river, past the place where they used to shoot the deserters, and on past the patches of maize and old Jonah's melon beds on the exposed areas of rich silt. All these familiar scenes I hoped never to see again.

Having made friends with my escort and crew, using my colloquial Turkish to some effect, I settled my few possessions conveniently on the kelek. I sat kicking my legs joyfully in the water, watching the kelekchis steer us out into the brisk current and away from the shoals and sandbanks as we rounded the many bends in the wide river. Mosul soon faded into the distance and, I hoped, into the past.

After a meal and an afternoon rest in my arbour, I felt like a swim. Easy enough, although I had to explain my intention to my two soldiers who at first viewed the project with surprise and suspicion. I just slid off the edge of the raft into the water and paddled around it in the current. This I did every morning and evening, to the great amusement of my companions.

Each night we tied up at established stopping places, usually near a village, where fresh produce could be bought cheaply. A fire built of brushwood made the campsite comfortable as the nights were as cold as the days were hot. Once or twice we passed through disturbed districts where hostile Arabs on the banks took pot-shots at us but my good kelekchis knew where to expect such compliments and steered well over to the opposite bank of the river. As we passed the mouths of the two Zab rivers, flowing into the Tigris from the east in a region of hot sulphur springs and shallow crude oil wells near Hammam Ali and Shergat, we saw lumps of pitch floating on the surface of the water, prophetic of the great oilfields near Kirkuk, as yet undiscovered. Going back in history, Noah's Ark, at the time of the Flood, was 'protected with pitch within and without'.

In this manner, as we drifted gaily down the sparkling river in perfect autumnal weather, I thought of Browning's *Wanderers*:

123

We set the sail and plied the oar;
But when the night wind blew like breath,
For joy of one day's voyage more
We sang together on the wide sea,
Like men at peace on a peaceful shore.

After all these years I can mock myself now as I recall how in my exuberant and optimistic mood, assisted perhaps by a noggin of raki, I sang, sotto voce, a brave passage from a then popular song: *Here in the morning of life I stand...*

For on my kelek I had my *Book of Verses*, my Loaf of Bread and even my Jug of Wine and only lacked some visionary 'Thou' beside me. There were, it is true, the kelekchis but their songs were in much more sombre vein. In their melancholy nasal quavering voices they sang of a lost love:

Sam'ra rafiq, oh! Sam'ra rafiq....
(Oh! my Samarra friend, my friend,)
where is she that I loved,
My Zubeida, my little dove,
Is she waiting for me when I come
Down to Samarra on my kelek?

I wonder if the kelekchis still sing this traditional old song or, indeed in this modern world, do the keleks still drift down the old Tigris from Mosul to Samarra and Baghdad?

Samarra, when we drifted past it, was lit up by a golden sunset glow which gave it an ethereal, magical look, its baked mud walls, turrets and towers and its slim minarets giving an illusion that it might be Petra, that 'rose, red city half as old as time', this fancy enhanced by a huge spiral ruin towering in the distance, reputed to have been the original Tower of Babel.

Our voyage lasted five days and, happy and content, we floated past the glorious mosque at Kaximain finally tying up our kelek at the appointed landing place in Baghdad.

Chapter Fourteen

Baghdad Rats

On reaching Baghdad on my raft at the beginning of December 1916, I was taken to see Cassim Bey, the Arab officer in charge of the prisoners of war depot, a man with a reputation for homosexuality and other venal vices but not hostile to the British. He examined my papers and accepted in principle that I was to be sent down river for repatriation as soon as it could be arranged. So far, so good.

After this interview I was given accommodation in a house overlooking the Tigris, on the right bank, just above the point where a railway siding ran from Baghdad station to a small wharf, a distance of about half a mile. In this house I found three or four British Kut men, detained in Baghdad for various reasons, and half a dozen others captured subsequently.

Once more, I found myself the only British officer in the place but there was an Afridi officer of the Indian Army who was suspected by the British soldiers of enjoying privileges from the Turks in return for political, subversive support. He was allowed a great deal of unexplained liberty and wore a version of a Turkish officer's headgear. This cap he promptly discarded on my arrival and resumed the correct kulla and safa he should have been wearing. His name was Cassim and he professed to be surprised that I declined to share a room with him or share his meals. He proved to be a thorough nuisance to me later on when we met again under conditions of great adversity, expecting me, when I was already exasperated with him, to make smooth his path when it was all I could do to keep myself going.

In the same house were a number of wretched Russian soldiers captured on the Persian front. We rarely saw them but heard them most nights singing their songs and choruses, their deep Russian voices booming and echoing up from their cellar below us. They had with them a little Lieutenant named Alexis; a sad, sensitive man, formerly a schoolmaster in the Ukraine who could have been a character out of Chekhov. He knew rather less French than I did but we exchanged surreptitious but unimportant notes. Later on, at the time of the fall of Baghdad, we met and had a serious conference. Already suffering from tuberculosis and therefore in no sort of condition for so severe a physical undertaking, he died on the march up country that followed the Turkish evacuation of the town. I was most thankful to find amongst the British prisoners a soldier named Laurence Eyres. He had been an undergraduate, in fact a scholar, at one of the Oxford colleges, had enlisted at the outbreak of war and gone through the Siege of Kut as a private in the Dorset Regiment. He had been retained in Baghdad by the Turks for clerical duties in connection with the prisoners of war. He became a schoolmaster in a well-known Catholic public school after the war.

Unlike me, he was a most ascetic character but, as I found him an amusing and intelligent compatriot to talk to after so many solitary days, I got him appointed as my orderly. On this footing he was allowed to come and talk to me whenever I wanted and each night we had games of chess, cribbage or bezique, or read poetry out of my Oxford book.

On the other bank of the river stood the Hotel Tigris (later the Hotel Maude) to which I was allowed to go twice a week to dine, guarded by a posta, after crossing the river in a boat. My usual boatman had two good eyes which distinguished him from nearly all the others, so that his Arabic name was the 'two-eyed boatman'!

The hotel proprietor was one Zia, a grand, convivial type who always treated me excellently. While my posta sat outside I used to go to Zia's office where he gave me a 'mezzeh' before dinner; lettuce, celery and cheese washed down with raki. As this liquor is very potent and was liberally dispensed, I was glad to find that a quantity of lettuce made an excellent antidote. I picked up bits of war news 'in code' from Zia who would hint that the weather downriver was good, or bad, to indicate how the battle was going. His sympathies were clearly with us.

At this hotel I was always waited on by Toma, the head waiter, even when the place was full of Turkish or German officers. One day I was brought a bottle of wine I had not ordered. I asked no questions but noticed that a Baghdadi at a table ahead of me was being served by Toma with the same wine. There was a large wall mirror in which we could see each other and when I raised my glass he did the same. It was in such cautious gestures that one came to recognize possible helpers. I learnt that the man owned a house and garden on the right bank in the southern outskirts and it was to this fruit garden, enclosed by a high wall, that I hoped to make my way if, at a suitable moment, an opportunity arose to give me the chance of slipping my guard, should my repatriation fall through. In this I was frustrated, as events turned out.

I found that Eyres was planning to escape with the aid of certain nuns who were trying to arrange for him to be smuggled away by some Christian Arabs and so I did what I could to encourage the project. I was not much interested for my own sake as I still had hopes that my repatriation would take place, receiving the usual regular assurances that I would be sent down river on the next steamer. In fact, I had just got my papers signed when, just before Christmas, General Maude commenced his fierce and methodical attack after months of inactivity. Because of this change in the tactical situation, my chance of exchange faded and eventually fell through. After this I took a keen interest in any possible scheme for escape but decided to wait until events downstream became clearer. Because I had not given any sort of parole in Baghdad, I was closely guarded the whole time. One evening, after a hospitable dinner at Zia's, I wanted to hijack the boat taking us back across the river, aiming to throw the boatman and the posta into the Tigris, but Eyres dissuaded me from what was a rather ill-considered scheme, pressing the point that they might be drowned!

127

We did go as far as working out a scheme of climbing out of the house at night and escaping over a wall, in fact we did a rehearsal one dark night and scaled the wall on to the railway siding after supplying the night-watchman on the wharf with a bottle of raki, on which he got very drunk. I remember how my heart went thump. After we had climbed back, we decided that the scheme was workable, subject to knowing that the British were really making progress advancing up the river. As far as we knew, Maude's army was still held up and we thought that there were several Turkish divisions defending the hundred or so miles we would have to traverse.

It was about this time that Akbar turned up in Baghdad. He had been the servant to one of the officers in the 48th Pioneers and was an engaging young Mohammedan sometimes used as a relief cook in the Mess, being free from the caste restrictions which hamper Hindus and which make it impossible for a man to undertake any work outside that of his caste. The exceptions to this are those of the lowest castes who are only permitted to do the dirtiest and most degrading jobs. In the Battalion we had a 'sweeper', a very good worker, who was ready to take on any sort of work if permitted. His chance came when, as a prisoner working on a railway construction project, by energy and initiative he raised himself to a position of responsibility he could never have reached in India.

Akbar was just such an opportunist. When in May 1916 I had been left behind in Mosul, Akbar had gone off with the rest of his group in the direction of Ras el Ain where he obtained employment with some Germans on the strength of his cooking. One afternoon in August 1916 while I was lying perspiring on the reed mat on my bed in the Mosul hospital, I was aroused by a persistent but quiet knocking at my door. In a bad temper at being disturbed, I opened the door and found Akbar standing there. I was even more annoyed to see him dressed up in a German follower's uniform and wearing a dirty white peaked cap with a little concentric coloured disc in front. However, Akbar's previous knowledge of my character, based on much campaigning experience, saved him from being thrown out, for he promptly presented me with a large and fragrant plum cake!

I decided that less summary treatment was called for. I admitted him to my room.

'Akbar', I began, 'what is this? Have you joined the deserters?'

'Your Honour knows that I hate the Germans. They are only pigs.'

'Then what are you doing in this rig-out?'

'The desert is a bad place', with a wave towards the west whither our hungry and ragged army had been driven, 'many are dead, more dying from lack of food and care. A man must get back to the English before winter or die in misery over there. My Germans are going to fight the Russians at Ravandooz. It is better to ride back with them and wait one's chance than run away as a poor starving hajji to be robbed and beaten by Arabs or perhaps caught and hanged by the Turks. The Germans know that an Indian is the best cook for them between Stamboul and Singapore, so I have charge of their kitchen. Allah, in his mercy, has given me a poor understanding and, (pointing to the cake) they sleep in the afternoons'.

I received several more brove cakes from Akbar in Mosul and enjoyed them greatly, knowing from whence they came. Then I heard that the Duke of Mecklenburg's Machine Gun Mission had departed for the Persian front and Akbar's visits to me ceased abruptly. One day in the following December 1916, after my return to Baghdad, I was having tea in my room in the prisoners' house, wondering if or when I would be sent down river. This led me to think of Akbar and to speculate on his fate and fortune in the months that had intervened. It seemed only natural that just then an Arab urchin should bring me up a note which read in broken English:

I have heard that Your Honour is in Baghdad. I am in prison. Can the Protector of the Poor get me out? Akbar.

This set me quite a problem and a challenge. Doubtless, I thought, knowing Master Akbar, he had been cast into prison for some good and sufficient reason and who was I, a fellow prisoner of war, to beg for his release? I decided to approach Cassim Bey, who I knew was vain and ambitious and, being a Baghdadi, might wish to improve his standing with us in case of a Turkish disaster. In fact, he later deserted to us. I therefore went to his office next day and, after the routine of coffee and enquiries about his health, he asked me what was the news, i.e. what did I want?

'Oh Cassim Bey', I replied 'I am in such a plight. My cook has been taken ill and there isn't another in the prisoners' house'!

'Aman, aman, effendim, neh yapalam? (what can I do)? There is only one man in Baghdad powerful enough to help me, now that the Vali Bey and Khalil Pasha have gone down to Baghaila with Herr Grossmann Pasha, and that is you: or perhaps the Gendama Commandani might help me'?

Now Cassim and the Chief of Gendarmes were enemies and jealous of each other's authority. The result was that Cassim bestirred himself and, having some hold over the prison governor, or possibly in exchange for some quid pro quo, he induced that official to deliver up Akbar, and Cassim sent him over to me. The outcome was that my cook (who rapidly recovered from his fictitious illness) regularly received the benefit of Akbar's well-known repertory of story telling, in the tradition of Scheherazade, whilst Akbar was occasionally allowed to make some of his famous cakes.

The roof of our house after dinner, with a moon over the river and a gentle breeze stirring the palm tops, was just the right setting for Akbar's yarns as he squatted facing the moon, with a bottle of raki rather nearer him than me, while I sat in a deck chair. How much of his narrative was fact and how much was borrowed from one of his famous stories I am not prepared to hazard, but it related to his recent sojourn in Kut which was now the frontline of defence by the Turks against General Maude's attacking army and went something like this.

Yakob was a simple man and, of course, he would have got me hanged instead of himself if he had the wit, poor fool. He did not know I had run away from the Germans and, being

130

a Christian, he believed me when I told him I was a poor date seller. So we went into partnership and shared a hovel in the ruins of Kut town, I taking the safer side under the wall for the British shelled and bombed us daily and Yakob lay, like dead, with fright. Allah is merciful and just! I had some maps and papers hidden in the ground under my mat, also some money given me to buy food for them by the Germans before I ran away. I had a poor pilgrim's cloak and turban and these were what I had used for disguise as I made my way down to Kut through Kirkuk and Hillah.

All this I could well believe, or most of it, for I had recently seen an Indian sepoy who had escaped and made his way from the Amanus mountains, a journey of 700 miles, dressed only in an old gunny bag.

After a short interval for refreshments Akbar resumed his tale:

In Kut I bought a stock of dates from an Arab merchant ('bought' may have been 'stolen'!) and Yakob and I regularly went down to the Turkish trenches to sell them to the soldiers. Of course, we used to get driven off and beaten but on quiet days, when there was not much firing going on, the guard would let us wander for miles all over the Turkish position provided I gave him a good lump of dates or some cigarettes or hashish. I pretended to be a bit mad but all the time I was looking out for a way to get across to the British side. One day I went a bit too far and a Turkish officer arrested me and sent me back into Kut where I was put in prison. Yakob came to see me there and brought me some food and my bedding. I told him he could have my side of our room in Kut where he would be safer from the shelling. A poor dull man, mashallah! He did not guess that the hut would be searched. When they did so, they found my German papers under his mat under the wall. That is why they hanged him that evening and only sent me back to prison here in Baghdad. Allah Karim!

Akbar did not seem ashamed of his shocking treachery. He had learnt to survive by his wits and it was useless for me to argue with him. When Baghdad fell to the British three months later, we were all bundled north again with the Turkish army in retreat so I lost sight of him, but I feel sure that he survived, probably in less discomfort than most of us. Perhaps he even did what I failed to do, regain his freedom by hiding in Baghdad until the British entered it.

Towards the end of February 1917 we gathered that the British offensive was going strong. Kut had been recaptured and the Tigris crossed at Shumran but we had no reliable news as to how far our forces had been able to advance. The Turks were known to be fighting strong rearguard actions under Khalil.

One day we were thrilled to see a number of our planes come over and drop bombs, some near the Citadel and others aimed at the railway yards quite close to us. The bombs were not large and did little damage but the attack produced a reaction in the ancient city out of all proportion to their military effects. We were by now strictly confined to our house and contact with anyone outside became almost impossible except through Cassim or the American Consul, Mr Brissell. I took the precaution, thank heaven, of sending to the latter some kit, including my two lovely saddle bag carpets which I still have, and my diary of the siege (now in the Imperial War Museum) plus a few notes of no military or political importance.

Then dramatically on the morning of 28 February 1917 we saw a regular fleet of small and large boats, including great, round and capacious guffas like huge salad bowls, making their way across the river to the wharf right under our noses where there was a siding leading to the railway station, all of them loaded with the Germans of the administrative branch, with quantities of kit and baggage.

We watched with growing excitement for it was obvious that the evacuation had started and that our moment for putting our escape plan into operation was upon us. Eyres and I determined to escape that night, taking advantage of the confusion around the wharf. But alas, a strong guard arrived during the afternoon and we were all transported across the river and thrown all together, including a dozen Russians, into a remote, dark and dismal room inside the Citadel, a real old-fashioned fortress

132

with enormous walls yards thick and with iron studded gates! Light was provided by a couple of smoky oil lamps and I alone had been allowed some help to carry the small amount of personal kit and bedding I was able to bring with me from the POW house; the others only had what they could carry, a blanket or two, a change of shirt and a share in some toilet articles. We were brought some food and were allowed, under escort, to go one by one to the primitive and stinking latrine.

During the night Alexis came to me and said that some of his Russians wanted to make an attempt to escape by overpowering our guard, which consisted of only two or three Arab soldiers at the door to our room. We held a council-of-war about this and I must say we all felt pretty desperate. We felt that we could easily have overpowered our guards but the chances were that the Russians would then have killed them. They would certainly not have had keys to the main gates and we were in the innermost enclosure of the Citadel. There were armed guards at all key points (properly so called) who would have had no scruples about shooting us down if we had already killed our guards, and possibly even if we had not! I persuaded the Russians to wait for a better opportunity which might easily present itself later when a collective or individual escape attempt might be made.

With hindsight, I think that moment might have been as we were being marched across the boat bridge at dawn next morning, when we might have jumped into the river and swum for it. The bridge was, however, right at the top of the town, so that even if one escaped being shot in the water there would have been a good chance of being recaptured during the long day ahead before darkness descended to hide us. I got as far as developing a problem with one of my boots, pretending to take it off to look for a stone, but being the only British officer, I was under special guard and soon got a dig from the butt of a bayoneted rifle to spur me on after the others.

So our desolate little company was herded out of Baghdad and off on the Mosul road again, with not even the prospect of a lift by rail as far as Samarra. We halted a while by the glorious mosque of Kakimain, the tomb of Imam Mousa, and it was here

133

that I decided to feign sickness, presenting alarming symptoms, falling down and clutching my stomach in agony and in the end getting myself sent back in a barouche to a hospital in Baghdad. The doctors there were sympathetic but I failed to convince them that I was ill. Next, I argued that, as I had been sent down from Mosul for the express purpose of being liberated, I should be allowed to stay with the American Consul. However, the hospital authorities were not prepared to admit that Baghdad was about to fall as no decision had as yet been taken to abandon it and I had no papers with me to prove my case for exchange. Even Cassim seemed to have disappeared. All argument failed and on the evening of 3 March 1917, I was sent over to Baghdad railway station to go, once more, by train to Samarra. Exactly a week later, on the night of 10/11 March 1917, the Turks withdrew from Baghdad. The British occupied it on 11 March.

Darkness was already falling when I arrived with my two guards in the marshalling yard at the station where, beside the passenger train on which I was to travel, there was an assortment of open trucks on a parallel railway line. It was a scene of much confused activity and noise, lit only by oil flares and pressure lamps on posts. Arabs, Turks and Germans were working furiously, in uniform and in civilian clothes, loading trucks in the sidings without much orderliness in preparation for the evacuation which was clearly hourly expected. I was wearing a khaki Burberry and an old topi, both rather anonymous articles of attire and I thought that, if I could only manage to elude my guard for a brief moment amongst the dimly lit groups of people milling around, I could fade away into the mud-walled lanes, gardens and palm trees by the river bank. Then, choosing my moment, I could swim and float down the river by night, lie hidden by day and so obtain my freedom! For years after that day I used to dream of what an exciting and hazardous week I should have had if only I had been able to slip my captors.

My guards took me to the train and put me in an empty compartment, one staying with me while the other went off. I chatted to him in my colloquial Turkish and he seemed a friendly fellow. The train was not expected to start until dawn and at about midnight I demanded that I visit the latrine. It is the universal and commendable habit in the East to use water for ablutions on these occasions. I had taken the precaution earlier of drinking all the water in my water-bottle and, as my guard conducted me to the station latrine, I shook it and handed it to him asking if he would go and fill it for me at a nearby stand-pipe. Would he or wouldn't he take the bait? My heart beat fast at this moment. He hesitated and I pressed a silver coin into his hand. He must have sensed my excitement, seized me by the arm and shouted at me to come back to the train. I failed to shake him off and then others came to help him and ignominiously dragged me back to the train, locking me in the compartment!

After this the guards were more vigilant and when, at first light, the train steamed north, every mile taking me further from the advancing British troops, my chances of escape seemed gone for ever. I huddled miserably in my corner, dumb with tears of rage and frustration, disappointment and despair.

Chapter Fifteen

Back on the Mosul Road

The journey of eighty miles to Samarra took twenty-four hours owing to the turmoil on the railway. Reinforcements for the front were mixed in confusion with withdrawals and evacuations, a tide of invalids going north encountering a wave of fresh troops making their way south, while at intermediate stations much work was going on in the preparation of defensive positions, a pile of picks and shovels here and a group of disconsolate wounded there. The terminal station at Samarra was almost as chaotic as Baghdad, with parks and dumps of war material and stores spread around without order so far as one could see, a couple of heavy guns towering over bales of dirty and discarded uniforms.

On the train I had felt the walls of captivity closing around me again. Having heard that the trench warfare in France was approaching stalemate, I could not guess at how long the war, and therefore my own captivity, would continue. The convict does at least know the length of his sentence and can count the days and months to his release. We prisoners of war felt that, through no fault of our own, the best years of our lives, with all the opportunities they could offer, were slipping by past recall.

Fortunately, the realities of the present journey drew me back into the present as I was passed from one guardian to another, coming into contact with a miscellany of Turks, Arabs, Kurds, Persians, Armenians and Jews, in fact with a great variety of what I cheekily labelled as the 'odds and sods' who for one reason or another formed the Turkish Army. Under the present stressful circumstances many of these individuals were highly suspect and unreliable allies of the Turks. A few could speak English, and several others, notably the Persians, could speak French, and as I was, at least by daylight, clearly British I was the object of some interest. I was drawn willingly into conversation with several of them, conversing in English, French or basic Turkish, as seemed appropriate or intelligible. Day to day Turkish is a simple language of regular syntax and by now I had acquired enough fluency in it to cover the essentials.

On leaving the train I was put under the charge of a Turkish Captain named Wedgi Bey who took me off with a few of his soldiers across the river to Samarra town. There was a length of decauville railway running from the station on the right bank down to the river's edge about a mile away, where there was a small quay used by country boats to ferry passengers, including us, across to the opposite bank. It was also used as a loading and unloading point for cargo from the large river steamers plying their trade with the north.

Wedgi seemed friendly, like nearly all Turkish officers I met, and he arranged for the transport of my modest baggage, consisting chiefly of a roll of bedding in which were packed a few spare items of clothing, and a mule pannier containing the rest of my possessions. I was no longer under close guard and was allowed to move about with only light supervision. This state of affairs resulted in my being approached by a number of individuals with vague hints (rather than definite proposals) for escape. They nearly all professed dislike or even hatred of the Turks and sympathy with the British, as exemplified by me. One handsome and colourful Kurd, an obvious subject for casting as a brigand, whose voluminous waistband was stuffed with pistols and daggers, offered to arrange my escape. Although eager to do so, I feared he might prove no more reliable than his own pistols when the time came for effective action. I was also suspicious that there might be 'agents provocateurs' trying to earn themselves some credit by trapping me and I believe that it is possible that I may have fallen into such a snare when we reached Samarra which, in the confusion which arose, might have cost me my life. I have already mentioned how Samarra in the evening light, as viewed from the west, looked like a dream city out of the Arabian Nights and so it appeared until we got close to its gate when its dusty drabness became evident. I had made friends with a doctor in the Turkish Army, an Arab whose home (he said) was in the town but who had friends and interests in Amara, far down the Tigris, which was of course in British hands. He confided in me that he was extremely anxious to get back to the other side of the war line and that he believed that he could arrange this through an influential Sheik who was reputed to have affected a passage for certain others desirous of such a transfer. The doctor led me to believe that it would greatly strengthen his chances of being accepted by the British, and gaining employment, if he turned up bringing with him a British officer whom he had helped to escape.

I professed to be only casually interested in the idea but went round to see him in his billet near the eastern (desert) gate of the town, accompanied by a posta guard. Beyond this gate, out in the desert about a mile away, were some old tombs and the remains of the old Tower of legendary fame. He further confided to me that horses were to be brought to these tombs after dark and that he would make his way there in Bedouin disguise. He pointed out that the walls of the town were in a dilapidated state, with several wide breaches, and that they were almost unguarded.

In the face of these disclosures I could no longer conceal my interest in the proposal that he should smuggle me out, disguised to look like an Arab, and that we should then ride all night into the desert with a guide who knew how to cir-cumnavigate the desert tracks in order to reach the rear of the British frontline. He indicated that I would be expected to pay him a liberal reward if the enterprise proved a success.

Without definitely committing myself to this alluring scheme (so far as I could afterwards recollect), I agreed to go round to have coffee with him after my evening meal at a local eating house. He told me that he would have Arab kit ready and, as he was a Turkish officer in uniform at the moment, he would be able to send my friendly posta off to get cigarettes to get him out of the way.

Well, I regret to say that it turned out worse than a flop! I must have been indiscreet at some stage, or possibly the attempted escape at Baghdad railway station had come to light and been exaggerated and that had made me a marked man, for before I had even reached the doctor's lodging I was arrested on a charge of attempted escape.

The result was that I was committed to the local jail where I found myself sharing by far the worst cell in which I had ever been with as fearsome a collection of ruffians as could be found in the Middle East; possibly excellent characters in their own way, but definitely not my type! Moreover, some of them seemed to be very gloomy and even terrified, casting themselves down every now and then in prayers and lamentations. These were, I gathered, deserters who had been caught and were expecting to be shot at dawn. I vividly recalled the scenes of execution I had seen from my hospital window when I was in Mosul. My imagination ran riot with very unpleasant thoughts. In Baghdad I had certainly been trying, however ineffectually, to escape and since then I had been seen talking, on several occasions, to a number of suspicious characters between Baghdad and Samarra. I knew from personal experience that junior Turkish officials had on occasions blindly carried out what they understood to be their orders, without bothering to seek the authorization of their superiors, even in cases where they might reasonably have had doubts.

In this black, filthy and verminous dungeon I feared that in the darkness and confusion likely before the dawn, only six hours ahead, some 'ghastly mistake' might get me included in the condemned squad. And even if this fate did not overtake me, I was only too aware that there was an epidemic of typhus locally and that this disease is conveyed by the bite of lice and other vermin, which, if not already advancing to attack me, would inevitably shortly make their activities felt. I decided that this jail was definitely not a healthy place in which to spend the night. Prompt and direct action was indicated!

139

Thanking God for my smattering of Turkish, I managed to bribe the jailer to arrange to send a note in French to Wedgi Effendi telling him of my predicament and requesting his intervention, promising a further reward if I got a favourable reply from him. Indeed, I staked my last golden pound on the outcome and was rewarded after one of the most anxious hours of my life by being brought out from the jail and taken before a senior Turkish officer. He severely interrogated me and I not only indignantly denied everything but protested most strongly about the treatment to which I had been subjected. I was then returned to my billet under my previous escorts, who were themselves petrified with fear since if I had escaped they would have had to answer for me. At sunrise next morning, as I heard a short fusillade of shots which came from under the city wall, I could not help picturing myself standing in front of those rifle muzzles if events had taken a different turn at midnight. What if I had been broke?

We left Samarra next day, re-crossing the river in dhows and loading our kit onto the small wagons of the decauville. The only working steam engine was at the far end of the railway station and so we had to haul our railway trucks up a slight slope with the aid of a few donkeys. Half way there, we met an engine hauling a small train coming down towards us on the single track! This nearly ended in a battle. The oncoming crew stoutly refused to reverse their train – perhaps the engine lacked a serviceable reverse gear – and so we had to unload our trucks, heave them off the line and then put the whole lot back after the other train had passed by, hooting at us in triumph. Meanwhile I sat nearby on the sand enjoying the comedy and the furious battle of words which rose from the protagonists.

On arrival at the station, I was immediately ordered by a senior Turkish officer to join a party leaving for Mosul. He seemed to be in a vile temper, probably having heard bad news from the Baghdad front. On asking for transport for my kit he replied that there was no transport and instructed me to carry my own kit. 'Anything you cannot carry, leave with me and reclaim it in Mosul'! My protests failed to move him and I felt that I was in no position to insist, being still on the defensive over the night's happenings. I had accumulated a few simple possessions in the past few weeks, extra clothes, a change of shoes and slippers, a couple of cooking pots and a small stock of tea and sugar, which were all contained in an old regimental medical pannier for transport on a mule, marked with a Red Cross. All I could do now was to select just the absolute minimum of necessities (plus my *Oxford Book of Verse* which I carried everywhere), dump them in my old sleeping bag, sling it over my shoulder and march forward. All else was gone. I was also cleaned out of cash except for a few piastres which were in my pocket. I need hardly say that I never saw any of my abandoned baggage again, the Turkish officer and his entourage having seen to that.

By this time I had learnt the lesson that it was unrealistic to expect the hard-pressed Turks to treat us, their prisoners, better than their own soldiers; or to embarrass their own frontline by providing us with facilities which their own troops lacked. At Mosul, and elsewhere, I had seen groups of their own soldiers, under an NCO, handed a wad of dates and a handful of their notorious army biscuits and told to 'get off', and off they would go singing their great marching song, 'Sol, sagh, sol, rubadubadub', left, right, left, out into the wide desert with no question of transport to the next staging post, their full military equipment on their shoulders, a hardy and cheerful lot for the most part.

So I marched off from Samarra station with my sleeping bag over my shoulder, accompanied by my escort, on the same old desert trail, heading away from the south and hope of escape and towards Turkey and the prospect of a long period in captivity. Although I was in much better condition than on the previous journey, I now had none of my own race for company or support.

After a few miles things took a welcome turn for the better. I fell in with a friendly Turkish officer and he soon offered to get someone to carry my load. When at last we reached Tikrit we found there a river steamer making its way up to the limit of navigability near Kalat Shergat. I camped myself down on the crowded deck and spent three highly diverting though rather

141

restless days there, hampered by the obvious consideration that, in the state of lawlessness prevailing, many of my fellow travellers were, like Autolycus, ready to snap up unguarded trifles, so that I had to sleep with my boots as a pillow and never dared let any of my last remaining treasures out of my sight or touch.

I remember leaning over the deck rail as we chugged slowly up the patriarchal Tigris River, reciting bits from my book and laughing at the predicament which had placed me alone in such strange and wild company. There was nothing to do on board but that did not worry anybody.

There was one especially noticeable character, an old Arab storyteller with a scraggy henna-dyed beard and a few discoloured teeth who sat cross-legged on the deck, becoming the centre of a small circle of listeners. He told his stories for hour after hour in harsh Arab speech, with many gestures, to the accompaniment of shouts of 'Wallah' indicative of amazement and delight as the more telling points of his endless narrative emerged. His single glittering eye fixed his listeners as did that of the Ancient Mariner.

Occasionally Arabs on the banks sniped at us and their fire was returned with an assorted museum of firearms more dangerous to the users than to the opponent. No one was ever hit, the marksmanship being more joyous than well-aimed. Once, a group of wild pigs decided to cross the river ahead of us but got frightened by the steamer, with the result that they drifted right alongside the ship in the strong current. This was the signal for everyone to rush to the side of the ship and let off his pistol or rifle at them in the water. The outcome was a lot of splashing and great mirth. 'Wallah'!

Another incident involved another steamer making its way up river on the same escape route as ourselves. We had only a limited supply of coal, which the Captain eked out with wood and brushwood collected from time to time from the shore to keep up the head of steam. I noticed that at night we never tied up near this other vessel, in fact we seemed deliberately to avoid being in its vicinity. However, one day when we reached a convenient bank and tied up, this steamer, which on this day

142

had been sailing astern of us, docked itself immediately ahead at a distance of only a few yards. The next thing that happened was that their Captain, a rough-looking type, boarded us with an armed party and demanded our coal. A heated argument followed and I almost hoped to see shots exchanged, but the pirate chief finally prevailed by virtue of the convincing argument of his superior firepower, going off with a large part of our precious stock of coal. I thought that our skipper would have a stroke at any moment!

We reached the archaeological excavations at Shergat a day or two later after much trouble with sandbanks and when it became evident that the steamer drew too much water to go any further. So we disembarked and my escort and I set off on the march once again. We were fortunate to have delightful spring-like weather and, as there had been a lot of rain, the whole desert was carpeted with wild anemones and other flowers. I happened to pick one or two, whereupon my friends and sym-pathizers embarrassed me by then presenting to me great bunches of flowers as we walked along. I found that I could not remain despondent when those around me seemed so kindly disposed towards the unlucky British doctor.

For the first part of this march I was attached, with my posta, to a brigade of Turkish heavy artillery. It was on its way to join von Falkenhayn's force, known as the Yilderim, at Aleppo which was unlucky enough to be overwhelmed during Allenby's successful campaign in the late summer of the following year. The two batteries were officered by Turks but the Brigade staffs were German and I had some fun playing off one side against the other, for I soon discovered that the Turks were jealous of the Germans and the Germans had a poor opinion of the Turks. My escort naturally took me first to the Turkish Officers' Mess, where I was kindly received and given a good meal. After some halting conversation in Turkish, mixed with French (why will foreigners always talk so fast!) the Battery Commander asked me if I had reported to the Brigade Colonel, a German, and when I replied in the negative, he sent me off to that officer's tent.

The man was a typical Prussian and received me very haughtily but later, having relieved his feelings, he relented and attached me to his German orderlies. These were a cheerful bunch and were quite ready to treat me well but as I was by now on my dignity after my interview with their Colonel, and as they and I had no language in which we could communicate, the relationship became a bit strained, so I obtained reluctant permission to return to the Turkish Battery where my language was understood. These German soldiers were musically minded and often sang on the march and did a sort of turkey trot.

On returning from the German camp, I was received by the Turks with even more friendliness than before, especially when I indicated that I preferred their company to that of the Germans. They were very upset that their two Batteries, commanded by senior and experienced Turkish officers, had been placed under a German who treated them as if they were beings of an inferior race. I did my best to play upon this feeling, pointing out that friendly relations had been traditional between our two races, and especially between the two countries' navies.

One day a Turkish officer gave me a ride on his charger while he took a turn marching beside me. Just then the German Colonel came dashing by accompanied by his staff, as was his wont. Seeing me on a horse he reined in spectacularly, roared for the Turkish officer and gave him a stern rebuke, the tone of which made me realize how suitable the German language is for use on such occasions, even when I did not understand a word of it. The meaning was crystal clear.

So I marched along to the tune of the Turkish marching song, 'sol, sagh, sol', back once again to the old barracks at Mosul, weary and saddened by the change for the worse in my fortunes since that happy day when I had sailed away, so full of hope, to the south on my kelek four months earlier. On reaching Mosul I learnt, with mixed feelings that Baghdad had fallen to the British a few days earlier.

Other brief memories of that march come back to me: the sight of the shallow pools near Hammam Ali covered with a thick scum of crude oil which, for many years, had been skimmed off as a commercial product for local use; a visit with Turkish officers to a tumbledown building at the same place for a dip in the hot springs arising there, too scalding hot and too sulphurous for comfort, but credited with therapeutic virtues; and, one night, listening to a little band of Germans, including a nursing sister, gathered together beside their camp fire singing their inspiring *Deutschland über Alles* under the bright desert stars, the dim outline of their parked field batteries and transport wagons surrounding them, just discernible in the darkness.

Chapter Sixteen

Into Anatolia at Last

The immediate impression I gained on my return to Mosul was that because of the dramatic ebb in the fortunes of the Turkish forces fighting on the Tigris, a wind of change had blown in from the south. Everyone I met, and all my old acquaintances, seemed to be depressed and there was an indefinable air of insecurity which pervaded the entire daily round.

This time, in place of the relative comfort and freedom of my room at the hospital, I was incarcerated in a small room on the gallery of the murky old caserne, in a room familiar to, and hated by, those who had been kept in it before, as was evidenced by the graffiti still legible on the white-washed walls. During the two days I remained in Mosul I was only allowed out twice a day, under strict supervision, for meals at the Club restaurant. The former Merkez Commandi, Umar Bey, was absent and his successor was noticeably uninterested in me, except for an obvious desire to get me away in the direction of Ras el Ain and off his hands. I was fortunately able to contact Enrico (God rest his friendly soul) and he cashed me a cheque, written out on a piece of letter paper, which was duly honoured after the war by my London bankers, and so was able to buy a few urgently needed items of kit and clothing. There was even a little left over to supplement an unexpected but providential issue of my month's prisoner of war pay of eight paper Turkish pounds.

Thus equipped and financed I turned my thoughts towards the long road before me across the deserts and mountains into Anatolia, that last 'home of the faithful'. I had heard no unbiased report of what I might expect on the route for I was the last of the Kut garrison to set out on the trail. The Turks, out of mistaken kindness, made out that it was a smooth, well-organized and carefree journey, adding significantly that I was privileged to leave after only a few hours delay.

I was glad enough to leave as I wanted to rejoin my comrades and friends and had no desire to remain alone any longer. There was nothing to keep me in Mosul. My wards in the hospital were long since empty of British or Indian soldiers and I had no friends to talk to.

I required little time to get ready for my journey and being told to be ready to move at dawn was no problem. Transport? Yes, some form of transport would be provided. This was a relief and I hoped that it might be an araba but when I was conducted out of the barrack gates early next morning I found a convoy of empty Austrian motor lorries drawn up in front of the square. They had come down from Ravandooz and in over the Tigris Bridge the previous evening. I was to be given a lift as far as Nisibin, perhaps even as far as the railhead at Ras el Ain. It sounded marvellous! A week's hard march was achieved in just a single day.

I was less well pleased to find I was to have as my travelling companion the Afridi officer of whose loyalty I was more than doubtful. He had now become tiresomely submissive.

Although I had no premonition of it on setting out, this journey was to be by far the most exhausting and uncomfortable of all my journeys and there were times during the next weeks when I thought I had reached the limit of human endurance; if I had not been thoroughly fit and possessed of good recuperative power, I believe I would have gone under as so many others had done. Physical exhaustion can be greatly exacerbated if mental strain is also present and what added to my trials was that the Afridi would talk to none but me, and his talk had to be in Urdu, a language as foreign to him as it was to me, his native tongue being Pushtu. Moreover, so far as it being in any way soothing or encouraging talking with him, his discourse consisted exclusively of grumbling and groaning about every-thing. He was incapable of doing anything for himself,

147

constantly getting himself into some dispute with our guards, at such times appealing to me as to God Almighty for intervention or assistance of one sort or another. If I had sufficient command of a common language in which I could have given him a really good dressing down it would have been as big a relief as when a thunderstorm relieves atmospheric pressure!

However, there was no help for it, for better or worse, we were stuck together till our long journey ended many days later at Kedos in the remote mountains of Anatolia.

Returning to the commencement of the journey, we stood together in the cool morning air, guarding our kits beside the line of Austrian lorries outside the gates of the caserne. After receiving the customary gifts and tokens of goodwill for the journey from some friends who had come to see me off, we clambered into the back of the last truck and sat hunched up, clinging to the sides while the empty lorry leapt and bounded along what seemed to be an endless track. This well used route was very rough and dry so that each vehicle raised a swirling cloud of dust which swept along with us and eddied back behind the driver's cab into the body of the truck, in what appeared to be a sinister attempt to suffocate us. Speaking for myself, I was soon denuded of skin on my legs as a result of heavy and unpredictable jolting, blinded and choked by the acrid dust and, before long, quite exhausted by the effort of holding on to the side of the leaping lorry. My Afridi was, poor wretch, in an alternating state of either being sick, with dismal coughs and groans, or passing out.

I usually enjoy travel, especially on the ground; there is usually something of interest to be seen as one passes along. But on this occasion I was too fully occupied with trying to mitigate present discomforts to take note of such things. We traversed a long stretch of undulating and barren land almost devoid of habitation before dropping down into more fertile country with occasional streams at which we stopped to fill up radiators. At these brief halts I was able to clear some of the dust from my sweating face and freshen myself up, though my eyes, nose and lungs remained full of the irritating stuff.

Some of these stopping places were in well-built but derelict villages with signs of recent cultivation in the nearby fertile fields. I soon found out what had caused this dreadful desolation. These had been Armenian villages in which there had been ruthless massacres carried out by the Turks a few months earlier. Dead bodies had been thrown into the wells rendering the villages uninhabitable. We passed through several such hamlets without stopping as fortunately we carried our own water supply. We were also told the horror story of the refugee camp for Armenians which had been established on the precipitous bank of the Euphrates near Jerablus whose inmates had been unwilling to cooperate with the authorities. When it became clear that the Turks could not supply food for them, all the old people were driven or thrown over the cliff into the river flowing below. I heard various versions of this story from different sources and concluded that there must have been much truth in it and the deserted villages bore witness to some such action. When I was in Mosul there was a miserable camp of Armenian women and children who were supported by the charitable members of the town. Those women who were able bodied, with the older children, were working as household drudges, practically as slaves. One old woman offered me her grand-daughter, aged about three, but in the circumstances of being a prisoner and a bachelor, I could do nothing to rescue the engaging child. I used to wonder what became of her.

But war is not all loss, even to those on the losing side. Perhaps this old woman gained some quality by her suffering, lacked by those who triumphed. Was it justifiable to place the boastful inscription on a 1914-18 war memorial at Hyde Park Corner beneath a graceful figure of David leaning casually on his sword? It reads, 'Saul hath slain his thousands but David his tens of thousands'.

Towards evening of this first day of my journey west, the wind changed and now that the ground was less parched the dust became less obliterating and I was able to get a pleasing impression of the little town of Nisibin, set on a low hill with a skyline of a ridge of higher hills behind it to the north. The town had neat, well-built houses with red tiled roofs instead of flat mud

149

ones and it had an avenue of poplars. The people wore western style clothes of good home-spun cloth giving the impression that the area was more Syrian than Mesopotamian. We stopped here for the night, camped beside our lorries; fires were lit and a meal prepared but I spent the night in poor shape coughing up the dust from my lungs, sore and weary from the 120 miles of buffeting and trying to cling on to the truck. I wondered if this form of transport was really an improvement on the old leisurely and colourful caravan such as I had seen in the market places of Amara, Baghdad and Mosul, where to attempt to maintain an exact timetable was considered great foolishness!

Next morning, seeking to put this philosophy into practice, I walked into the peaceful and orderly little town to do some shopping, only to be hastily recalled with shouts of 'Yallah', (hurry up), and was bundled speedily into my lorry again.

Ras el Ain, which we reached after a short morning run, was a large and straggling camp, shapeless and without any redeeming feature. It marked the eastern terminal of the section of the Baghdad railway which ran from Syria and thus, in theory, was the goal towards which our unfortunate prisoners from Kut had struggled the previous summer through nearly 500 miles of deserts. If any one of them had hoped to find here a well-built and finished railway station, with a restaurant, waiting rooms and the other facilities commonly expected, he was doomed to disappointment, for all that there was to see was a great long dusty camp with even more legions of flies than elsewhere.

A double line of rails ran for a short distance before terminating feebly in the desert sands, just as the other end of the line did at Samarra, as if they were too spiritless to drag themselves further. There were irregular dumps and pyramids of railway and military stores and materials, many goods wagons, open and covered, with two or three smoky and fussy little shunting engines push-and-pulling them about. Often these engines stood unused, serving solely as a source of hot water to make tea or coffee for the engineer and his friends. During the course of my subsequent rail journeys I learnt that I could always get my hot water for washing and shaving from this source.

Also to be seen were droves of mangy and downcast donkeys and a few disagreeable looking camels with their Arab attendants. But what gave me a thrill was to see groups of our sepoys working in gangs on or near the railhead.

As it was now nearly a year since we had been captured, these represented the stalwarts, the tough survivors, the 'he that endureth to the end' types. They were good workmen, well trained by the Indian Army and used to hardship and discipline and in consequence the Turks had found it to their advantage to feed and shelter them adequately. All the way onward from Ras el Ain, along the railway and through the Toros mountains, wherever construction work was being done to link up the new line with the regular Anatolian Railway system at Posante, gangs of our men were seen to be at work.

Since at this time this was essentially a military railway, it may seem questionable whether it was permissible to make POWs work on it but at least it must be said that it served the men's best interests. It saved them mentally and physically from the inertia and boredom liable to affect those who have no interests and it was the means of their obtaining better and more considerate treatment than was given to those found unfit or unsuitable for work who were segregated into enclosed camps. Moreover there was the additional incentive that ability and hard work was rewarded with extra privileges and responsibilities.

In these respects I believe that many of us in Turkey, provided we survived the earlier and severest stresses, suffered less than those imprisoned in Germany. For although the final camps in Anatolia were real prison camps causing their inmates great but varying hardship, there were those like myself who, for much of the time, were not held in prison camps but were moving about having to fend for ourselves and use our wits (and perhaps a bit of skulduggery at the Turks' expense). We had a healthier lifestyle and not only gained material advantages but also some psychological tonic which stood us in good stead right up to the end of our captivity.

During my protracted journey I saw here and there gangs of Russians working on the railway and it struck me that they appeared to be treated considerably more harshly than were our own people. The Turkish attitude towards the Russians was interesting. For centuries war between the two countries had been common. They had much experience of each other's behaviour under the stress of war. When asked for their opinion of the Russians, my Turkish acquaintances' comment was always 'Muscovi barbar'! Their opinion was, of course, biased and perhaps there was not a lot to choose between them.

Although it will be gathered that Ras el Ain did not rouse in me any desire to linger, I have one vivid and surprising memory of it, like a shaft of sunlight piercing a stormy sky. Hot, sore and very dirty, grimly aware of the sticky and disgusting state of my shirt and trousers; I asked to be allowed a wash. They took me to a place, about half a mile away, where there were three pools, in series, of varying size, rising from springs from which the place gets its name. Utterly unexpectedly, I found these pools, especially the furthest one, filled with dazzling clear water. The bottom of each was hard and white, with natural shallows and undulations. The water sparkled in the sun as I hastily undressed at the edge of the furthest and most crystal clear pool. The water was cool and utterly refreshing as I plunged into it and swam lazily about. Looking down, through ten feet of water I could see my own shadow outlined in the white screen below and I could even see the shadows of a shoal of fish as they darted too and fro. Enough time remained for me to wash my clothes and put them to dry on a rock in the sunlight whilst I indulged in a second swim in the caressing water.

One of the minor difficulties while on the move was to get one's clothes washed. Those of us taken at Kut were better off than those overrun in battle who were faced with journeys of days or weeks with nothing but the clothes they were wearing at the time. We at least had a change of shirt and could wash and delouse one (a game one became expert at) while we wore the other. On my present journey, I had practically no change of clothes, so put my shirt and trousers on before they were dry. For several weeks I did my own laundry, such as it was, and at times my own cooking. *A la guerre comme a la guerre.*

My halt at Ras el Ain was just long enough for news of my

arrival to be passed among the sepoys working on the railway line before I was put on a train for Aleppo next morning. My old friend, the Quartermaster Havildar of the 48th, heard that I was almost destitute and suddenly appeared at the window of my compartment where I was crowded in alongside my posta and my Afridi (more pathetic than ever). He flung in a large bundle containing shirt, socks, shorts and a few other items, including a small cooking pot, all done up in a blanket. Each and every one of these gifts was of the greatest value to me in the months ahead. A final surprise came when, just as the train started, a large uncooked fish came hurtling through the window!

The fact that Quartermasters can usually lay their hands on almost anything has been a standard joke for centuries in all the armies of the world. It was the one unfailing stock item in the repertory of all ENSA comedians, always good for a laugh! I am sure it dates back to Roman times and even to when Alexander's Macedonians came storming through those Cicilian Gates in the Toros which I was shortly to traverse (though in the opposite direction).

On this occasion, so far from viewing with sanctimonious disapproval the dubious fiddling that had probably been called into play, I accepted the Quartermaster's largesse with avaricious gratitude.

In due course (that is to say after long inexplicable delays at unlikely spots), we arrived at Aleppo after crossing the Euphrates at Jerablus. I was put in a rundown hotel of which I can only remember that it was kept by a frightened Armenian, that I was locked in because I objected to the posta and the Afridi sharing my room, and that the army of bugs ran up the wall in order to drop more easily on to my bed!

Next day we moved on again by train in a third class old wooden coach, crowded with Turk and Arab soldiers. My fellow travellers smelt abominably and seemed to prefer sleeping in a flopping position supported by me. The three days it took to reach the foot of the Amanus Mountains were a nightmare and most exhausting. The only relief we got was when, as we slowly struggled up the low gradients, the poor overtaxed engine ground to a halt for lack of steam pressure.

Then, all the third-class passengers, including myself, descended and scoured the hillside for anything that would burn, chiefly brushwood or even reedy grass. Thus replenished, our engine would give a cautious whistle, we all clambered back aboard raising a cheer as we slowly got under way to cover a further couple of miles or till the welcome relief of a level stretch eased the strain on the suffering mechanism.

Further up in the mountains there was a big camp holding the German and Swiss engineers supervising the railway work and constructing an immense tunnel and a fine bridge across the gorge. We traversed the tunnel in pitch darkness, being drawn through by a mysterious sort of engine with a long cylindrical body without a funnel or firebox, charged I suppose with compressed and super-heated steam from a steam-raising plant nearby. The air in the tunnel was fresh, cool but muggy. Finally we emerged at a large camp at Mamouri, high up on the mountains where the scenery was very pleasing rather than sensational.

My memory of the rest of the journey is very jumbled and vague. It took many days, through the Toros Mountains and the Cicilian Gates and so ultimately down to the Anatolian plain at Posante. I marched many of these stages, often by choice, but had some form of transport for my kit, usually a mule cart.

Other towns en route included Adana, Tarsus (said to be the birthplace of St Paul), and Konia, an important town and railway junction. I slept in dirty little hotels or on the station platforms and got meals at small locantas, with plenty of good fruit. I was often too tired to sleep because I never got a proper night's sleep on a comfortable bug-free bed. The worst night was with about thirty Turkish soldiers in one of those trucks labelled *'huit chevaux ou quarante hommes'*. No one had bothered to clean it since its *'huit chevaux'* days and it was full of fleas. The big doors were, of course, shut and barred and the only light came from two small barred windows high up but fortunately devoid of glass. In this loathsome vehicle the only consolation with which I could find any comfort was that we were moving – at least part of the time!

And so we passed through Karaman:-
Thy hundred hills, thy thousand streams
Karaman, O Karaman!
The hot bright plains, the sun, the skies,
Karaman!....blood and bones of slaughtered men,
Karaman!

Neither did I see much of Afion Kara Hissar, where a stupendous near-vertical black rock, rising abruptly from the plain, gives its name to the town sheltering below. Here was the principal prisoner of war camp for British soldiers where the Commandant had a particularly evil reputation for cruelty and vice. There were no officers held at Afion and I was told my destination was a place called Kutahieh, a most rosy picture being painted of it. According to this account, most of the Kut officers, except the most senior, were living here in luxury. Knowing the British addiction to football, this sport was mentioned as a notable attraction. Anxiously looking forward to the end of my long period of travel, overall a distance of 2,500 miles since I left Kut, I foolishly believed at least part of the fable.

In the event, due to typical Turkish incompetence, it turned out that Kutahieh was exclusively a camp for Russians and I found myself lodged with them for three days before things were sorted out. The Russians treated me with kindness and with respect as well as with surprise, and possibly a little suspicion at my being planted in their midst. So far as I remember, neither they nor I were really aware of the revolution that had just taken place in their country or of its implications in international affairs. They had, I presume, no potential Lenins lurking in their midst and I had not been sent to uncover his machinations. I did, unwisely, engage in a couple of games of chess with them, the only medium of contact between us, and rapidly got humiliating defeats. It is after all their national game! I should have taken them on at football.

After an exchange of telegrams, my correct destination was ascertained; for Kutahieh read Kedos, a hundred miles further on across the mountains, but all the other Arcadian features were understood to hold good. I would find at Kedos every-

155

thing the heart could desire, play football all day with my fellow officers and, in fact, live in idleness and comfort till the end of the war! What more could I desire in life? It seemed to be a source of unending surprise to the Turks that we, as prisoners, should be dissatisfied with our lot. It seemed to them strange that young and healthy British officers should look for some outlet for their mental and physical energies. These are the energies which have inspired, under conditions of captivity or imprisonment, almost every attempt to escape, even the most foolish ones.

Apart from the fact that Kedos* really was my final destination, there was scarcely a word of truth in their description of it. I think that my Turkish informants did not mean to deceive me so much as cheer me up, seeing that I was cynical and depressed by continual hardships and misfortunes.

*At that time, when Arabic script was used, the western equivalent was either Kedos or Gediz and we were instructed to use the former spelling. Under Mustafa Kemal's reformed script the name became Gediz. The town was totally destroyed by an earthquake in March 1970 with heavy loss of life.

Chapter Seventeen

Kedos Camp under Dippy

For my last night in Kutahieh I was allowed to stay at a large khan or serai in the town, a sort of coaching station, before starting my journey over the mountains which commenced very early next morning. This khan was one degree better than some I had stayed at and I could well have borne it with fortitude had not the Afridi got himself involved in some dispute with the kanchi just as I was settling down to sleep on the matting floor. They were shouting and gesticulating at each other but making no progress, one in Turkish, the other in Pushtu. Neither could I settle the matter when appealed to by both, as I really could not make out what it was all about, but I did get them to pipe down after a while, though they continued to snarl at each other like a couple of angry dogs held forcibly apart. My companion did not realize how near I came to murdering him and flinging his body down into the courtyard below!

The morning was bright and cool and reason appeared to have prevailed as we set off in style in two arabas. This was not a special favour as it was part of a regular transport service between Kutahieh and Kedos. We had a couple of other passengers and some baggage, parcels and baskets for transit.

These arabas were four-wheeled vehicles, light and springless, but with the flat floor behind the driver's seat covered by a mattress and a thick felt cloth. As I had acquired a cushion for a pillow I alternately sat up or stretched out without discomfort, protected from the sun and rain by the hooped hood. Each araba was drawn by a couple of small stallions.

We soon began to ascend into the pine-clad mountains on a rough stone road which was in pretty poor condition. This was my first real view of the highland scenery of central Asia Minor, with its pleasing alternations of rocky gorges clothed with pine trees and more rounded hills, where the slopes were terraced for vineyards, olive groves and fruit gardens, each with its red tiled small house and sheds. There were also wide stretches of alpine grasslands mottled with flocks of sheep and goats.

At the higher levels the smoke of the charcoal burners floated above the pines and there were attractive little wayside streams and springs just in the angles where one would expect them.

The dusty road wound gradually upwards as we left the pastures and reached the wooded gorges, our ponies urged on by occasional blood-curdling threats and profanities to which their response was perfunctory and short lived. Nonetheless we made steady progress, stopping every few miles at small khans or coffee houses in the villages where the arabachis were well known and evidently popular as purveyors of local news and gossip. As usual, I was the centre of much interest, especially to the numerous bright-eyed children who crowded round us. My attempts at conversation in Turkish caused them much merriment.

Just before sunset we reached a khan on the outskirts of a large village high up in the mountains, driving in through an archway into the central courtyard where stabling and fodder were made available for our ponies.

These khans are like small forts and the strong iron-studded doors are shut and securely bolted at dusk in times of trouble, a reminder that brigands and outlaws, often deserters from the army, were not unknown in these deserted highlands. There were also a number of young men – later I met several – who, with the connivance of the villagers, were evading military service. Up there, where life was hard, strong young arms, active legs and unbent backs, to say nothing of gay spirits, were not to be surrendered lightly to distant campaigns from which so many did not return.

There was a cheerful wood fire on the wide stone hearth where we all sat round on mats eating a rice and mutton pilau with our fingers out of a common trencher and drinking water from the mountain stream from an earthen pitcher. The light from the fire was supplemented by the feebler but steadier glimmers from wicks placed in a number of small bowls of baked clay, such as are found in any museum of medieval culture. These wicks burnt poppy-seed oil and, as no one in such company would wish to read except by daylight; a desire for any brighter source of light would have been regarded as eccentric.

Having shown that we were replete in the accepted manner, and drunk numerous little glasses of coffee, we lay down in a line on a raised wooden platform covered by a reed mat and a few well worn kilims situated along one side of the room, having wrapped ourselves in whatever rugs, blankets or coats we possessed. We were soon asleep, mercifully not tormented here by insect horrors because of the colder air up in the mountains. It is not difficult to sleep face downwards even on a stone hard flat floor but it is easier in the desert where you can hollow out holes to fit your elbows, hip-bones and toes.

Before dawn we were all stirring and, while a meal of 'bulgur' – boiled wheat grains – and tea was being prepared, I made my way out in search of a wash. Close by I found in the angle of the road a convenient water trough made out of a hollowed-out tree trunk, fed by a spout from the rivulet coursing down the hillside. I certainly surprised and, perhaps, shocked the onlookers by taking a dip, a most refreshing one, and followed it by a good wash and shave in expectation of meeting my British friends that evening in Kedos.

Soon we were on the road again, gradually descending among the fertile and peaceful hills as the road wound downwards. Towards evening, I received the exciting news that the little town nestling in the valley below was indeed Kedos, and warmed myself with the thought of the welcome I expected to receive from the many old friends I would doubtless meet there.

Gaily we swung down the road for the last mile, our ponies well aware that the day's run was almost over. Between us and the town ran a stream and, just short of the stone bridge crossing it, we turned in at a gateway on the right of the road and pulled up by a miniature garden with roses on a pergola and with a little summer house in its centre, close by the bank of the stream. On our right were three good buildings in line, comfortably sheltered under the hill and a clump of trees, all that represented the famous 'football ground' I had been promised. Half a mile away, across the stream, one could see the two minarets of the town, with its streets of houses constructed, fatally as it turned out, almost entirely of wood. All promised well, or at least promised a vast improvement on the past few months.

But where were the other prisoners? I looked for them in vain and questions formed in my mind. Perhaps it was the time of their evening meal and they were all in the big two-story building a hundred yards away. Quite imposing it looked. I felt hungry and I hoped I would be in time to join them and exchange greetings and news. Would they be expecting me or would it be a surprise?

Our vehicles drove in and our ponies, sweaty and dusty after their long and helter-skelter descent from the mountains, pulled up close to a rustic gate leading to the little garden on our left. Suddenly, as we jumped to the ground, there came charging out from the barrack building, the centre of the three, half a dozen elderly Turkish soldiers, led by a Chaoush (Sergeant). We were immediately surrounded by these characters, each pointing a musket of sorts at us, each with an evil looking bayonet fixed to the muzzle. They evidently thought that their chance of martial glory was at hand and were prepared to plunge into immediate action if we should make the slightest move. Our pathetic baggage was unceremoniously unloaded from the arabas which promptly drove off into the town and were seen no more.

It was at this moment that I began to have serious misgivings and wonder if this was not after all the Mecca I had expected at the end of our long and exhausting journey. The date was 27 April 1917, only two days less than a year after Kut had fallen. The journey from Baghdad had taken eight weeks.

We stood for a short time surrounded by a ring of steel, but were not in the least daunted by it because our captors looked a bit silly, particularly as they tried to look valiant, when there emerged from the summerhouse the strange figure of the Commandant, Habib Nuri Bey, wearing the epaulettes of a Lieutenant Colonel in the Turkish Army.

Habib Nuri was an Albanian by birth, as he proudly announced on many occasions. This boast, combined with the obvious fact that he could never aspire to command in the field, seemed to be his sole qualification to justify his appointment to administer a camp for British officer prisoners of war.

Habib Nuri was a very undersized man, slight and short, who further reduced his height by stooping and hunching his shoulders. His face was excessively wrinkled and this effect was increased because his usual expression of intense irritation made him look like an angry weasel. I think that he probably suffered from a gastric ulcer! Under his drooping moustache, his slobbering lower lip hung down, or was drawn down in a sneer, exposing his few irregular and discoloured teeth. On the rare occasions when he chose to be extremely affable, his face developed an inane leer which was even more fascinating than his customary expression.

Below his military cap and shabby tunic, unbuttoned at the throat, he wore a pair of uniform trousers made for a much taller man, so that they fell like a concertina round his slippers. The sling of his sword was also too long so that the weapon's tip trailed on the ground and occasionally tripped him up! Often he would appear without his cap, his scrubby white hair testifying to its lack of recent acquaintance with brush and comb. The town barber came to shave him twice a week. Later, when more officers arrived at the camp and his character was more closely observed, he was given the nickname 'Dippy Dick' or more simply 'Dippy'.

On the present occasion this grotesque personage desired first of all to impress on us and on his subordinates his standards of military discipline and efficiency. It also gave him the opportunity to satisfy his never failing curiosity on the subject of our personal effects, though to give him his due this curiosity never developed into acquisitiveness. My own kit, apart from a scanty supply of clothing and bedding, consisted of a small saucepan, tin cup, knife fork and spoon, razor and toilet minima and one book. The knife, razor and book were at once impounded but I was allowed to keep the fork, with evident misgivings. The book had to be sent to Constantinople to be censored and was returned to me six months later bearing identifying details and the censor's stamp, in Arabic characters, which it bears to this day.

Nuri and I then had a prolonged discussion, in bad French, from which I gathered the following:

a. There were as yet no prisoners in the camp! It had been fully staffed, awaiting 'customers' for three months.

b. I could have a loaf of bread daily at military rates.

c. My requirements about other supplies would be fully satisfied in the morning!

d. I would be allowed my razor for a few minutes daily. He obviously thought this very faddy.

e. As he was now due for his evening meal, we were to go to our allotted quarters.

He then tottered off and we were marched away at bayonet point to the big barrack building and locked in with great ceremony. This barrack block had been built as a clothing depot but had not been used and was substantial and clean. It comprised two large rooms, in one of which we were confined, a small kitchen, an earth latrine downstairs and a small set of rooms on the top storey. There were neither fittings nor furniture and no arrangements for lighting except for an oil lamp which was removed one hour or two after dark. As I had expected to come to an established camp I had brought no food except for a small amount of tea and sugar. We were each given a loaf of good wholemeal bread and made a meal of part of that with a drink of water brought to us in my cooking pot from the water spout on the hillside behind the barracks, by one of the postas. This cooking pot had to serve as washbasin, water container and cooking vessel for several days during which time we had no furniture except a small wooden bench borrowed from the Turks.

The Commandant inspired such terror amongst his staff by his unaccountable rages, (I saw him on one occasion strike the Chaoush across the face while the latter still stood at the salute), that until he reappeared on the day after our arrival, towards midday, we were kept locked in our room, hungry, dirty and exasperated after an uncomfortable night on the bare boards.

It was then that I had the first of many flaming rows with him which always ended in both of us losing our tempers and becoming more and more incoherent as we assailed each other in a futile mixture of my elementary Turkish and his bad French. The usual result was that Nuri would stalk off, purple in the face with fury, leaving me on the barrack steps pale with frustration. He would soon return smiling with an excess of affability, present me with a rose and proclaim *'Je suis comme votre pere'*! I was alternatively, *'Bon officier'* or *'Monsieur le Docteur, comme la bete feroce'* and he was either my father or *'Je suis commandant du place'*, furious and ungrammatical. And so I remained for the next two weeks, angry and alone but:

> ...still nursing the unconquerable hope
> still clutching the inviolable shade.

I was not at all downcast, far from it. Heroics are unfashionable these cynical days, but deprived of any reading, I found some solace in writing on the whitewashed barrack room wall Henley's famous lines, for I often felt I was indeed 'in the fell clutch of circumstance'.

There was a house a short distance away towards the town and I noticed that whenever I took my daily walk to and fro on the meadow in front of the barracks, a girl appeared at one of the upper windows. Of course I pictured her as divinely beautiful and when I was taken to the shop in the town she let me have a glimpse, and was there a smile, before hastily withdrawing. It cheered me up but I regret to say that the romance never got any further! Under those circumstances any such incident becomes significant.

Another way of spending the time was to draw on a wall a picture of a fountain inspired by the song from 'Maud':

> Now sleeps the crimson petal, now the white,
> Nor waves the cypress in the palace walk,
> Nor winks the goldfin in the porphyry font.

This masterpiece I surmounted with the figure of a cherub, overlooking the fact that at that time the portrayal of the human figure, especially unclothed, was forbidden by Moslem rules. It was ruthlessly obliterated and for days I felt resentful after this unnecessary act. However, I had gained relief in that the Afridi had been removed to another abode and thereafter I saw him no more. More soothing was the piping of a simple tune on a rustic flute by a shepherd lad on the hillside behind the barrack and the sound of the water splashing from the spout that supplied us with water for all our purposes.

One day the friendly Chaoush told me that other officers were expected and this was confirmed when Habib Nuri visited me and directed me to concentrate my possessions, by now increased by purchases in the town, into a carefully marked out area of the barrack floor. The guards were also paraded, put through their paces and their arms checked and, sure enough, that evening three officers arrived who had been captured on the Baghdad front. A few days later others joined us from that front and from the fighting at Gaza. They were all practically destitute, dressed only in what they had been wearing when they were captured. Luckily it was summer. I had little to offer them but the first three were fortunately able to share a bottle of whisky I had acquired in the town, reputedly the last bottle in Kedos, but good pre-war whisky. Full of his own importance, Nuri issued, on loan, another cooking pot and authorized the issue of a few items of rations on repayment until we were able to get a regular Mess going by local purchase.

Money became more accessible once a system of cashing cheques through the American Express Company in Constantinople was organized. Soon local traders set up a market at the camp gate selling local produce which, at that time, was cheap and plentiful. A few of the eggs on sale had been long overlooked in some local farmyard and had the unpleasant characteristic of exploding violently when cracked! For many years after the war ended I remained cautious when cracking eggs. We also became wary of a sinister sort of cheese in a pot which, after purchase, bred an alarmingly athletic maggot that arched itself in a bow and fired itself at you in a most disconcerting manner. We set up a roster for cooking and as a result the daily menu became more varied, some 'cooks' attempting nothing more difficult than boiled eggs, whilst others excelled at producing Irish stew. We had no servants or orderlies until much later and no furniture beyond the original small bench and a chair or two bought in the town, with not a bed between us. I slept in a string hammock, to my mind a very uncomfortable contrivance, but at least it did not harbour bugs. A young Armenian named Antanric organized a laundry service, provided other simple services and, by his enterprise, built up a profitable business.

Nevertheless this improvement in our status had to be set against our increasing exasperation with the behaviour of the unpredictable 'Dippy'. One day, when I was shopping in the town with my guard, we met him and he appeared to have forgotten that he had given me permission to carry out this necessary task. He assaulted the posta and sent us both packing back to the barracks. Yet within minutes he turned up again as mild as milk and proceeded to take me down to the shops, making my purchases for me at a price considerably less than I would have had to pay on my own.

Some of our complaints were trivial but related to actions done on Dippy's behalf which added to our physical discomforts. For example we had obtained a pack of cards with which we played bridge and *'vingt et un'* but Dippy then ruled that this was illegal gambling and must stop. He had a mysterious book of rules from which he constantly quoted but would never produce. I believe it had been intended to regulate civil prisons and lunatic asylums. Then we made a set of chess men but at a critical stage in one game a posta intervened, or attempted to, so I pushed him away. For this crime I was imprisoned for a day on bread and water. On another occasion the senior British officer got three months' solitary for writing a strong complaint against Nuri in a letter home. There were other senseless stupidities, so we all sacrificed one of our two permitted monthly letters in order to write to the Red Crescent, the Dutch Ambassador or the Inspector General of Prisoner of War Camps in Constantinople asking for an inspector to be sent down. We were still without furniture, nor were we allowed to make any, in case we used the tools for some other desperate purpose!

In anticipation of an official inspection, we prepared a list of complaints and suggestions, including a demand that the Camp Commandant be replaced. It is a fact that in other camps in Turkey where serious complaints were made, in every case the Commandant was replaced by one who was a great improvement on his predecessor.

Chapter Eighteen

Better Days at Kedos

About the end of June 1917, old Nuri came to the barracks wearing his smarmiest smile and presented roses to the Senior British Officer and myself, at the same time announcing the relaxation of a couple of irritating though minor restrictions. He also suggested that we hold a sing-song that evening, although he had on previous occasions complained of the noise when we had held impromptu sing-songs. He was dressed more smartly than usual and he had the guard drawn up in a line by his rose garden, to which he then retired.

Shortly afterwards a smart carriage drove in and a tall and distinguished military officer descended from it. The guard presented arms and, wonder of wonders, our long awaited Inspector from 'Constantinople', Colonel Yusuf Zia Bey arrived.

He spent the first hour in the administrative block and then came with Nuri to the barracks where Major P and I were ready to receive him, armed with our memorandum. We were relieved when he sent Nuri away to his garden where he, Nuri, was seen to unbuckle his sword and fling it to the ground in an 'I will soldier no more' gesture.

Colonel Zia was astonished to find us without furniture and, when we offered to make our own tables, benches and beds, he sent at once to the town for saws, planks, nails etc. He allowed us to take over the small rooms upstairs and gave us the free run of the whole enclosure, including even the rose garden (but later Dippy, in tears, asked us to let him keep this). In fact, Colonel Zia created consternation in the Commandant's office, sacking on the spot a half-witted weedy subordinate named Ali who had plagued us. His visit produced jubilation in our barracks where saws and hammers were soon at work and we were then far too busy to oblige Nuri by providing him with a sing-song.

Next, half a dozen British orderlies arrived from Afion; a great improvement for them though there was not a lot they could do for us except take over the cooking. One had been a chef at the Savoy, but he found that his specialized talents were frustrated by only having the use of our charcoal braziers and the provision of limited foodstuff.

Parcels and letters from England began to arrive late that summer and I heard news from home for the first time for nearly two years. At about the same time, a new Commandant arrived to take over from Dippy who, not surprisingly, was not accorded a farewell party or a presentation from us! The newcomer, Edhem Bey, was a success with us from the start, a good-looking married man with, it was rumoured, a most attractive daughter. Although he could speak no language but Turkish he was always ready to listen to us and to enquire into our opinions with the aid of the interpreter who accompanied him and he treated us as reasonable beings.

There was no dentist in Kedos but there was a Greek at Ouchak, a day's journey away, who could do fillings and extractions. There were also in Ouchak a number of French 'ladies', exiles from Constantinople, living in a house. One or two of our younger and more frivolous officers found out that these same ladies were large hearted and, in the true spirit of Guy de Maupassant, delighted to entertain members of the Allied Forces in a pretty literal get-together! Quite an epidemic of toothache ensued but sadly the Greek dentist put a stop to that by arranging to come to Kedos once a week!

There was supposed to be a Turkish doctor at Kedos but he was very old and useless so when an Indian officer, living in a house in the town with several others, developed a liver abscess, I attempted to deal with it with a razor, a pair of nail scissors and a teaspoon. There was no chloroform and inadequate dressings. The result was far from satisfactory and when news of the affair reached England there was quite a stir in Parliament which resulted some time afterwards in the provision of better Turkish facilities. All this time I was being treated as an ordinary prisoner of war. I had no drugs or instruments, nor even the authority to treat anyone. In my exasperation and frustration, I submitted that, as I was not being used as a medical officer, I wished to call attention to the order passed by Khalid Pasha which had authorized for me to be exchanged across the frontline on the Tigris the previous Christmas. I subsequently heard nothing in reply for almost another year when, just before the end of the war, there was a surprising sequel.

The interior of Asia Minor is very mountainous and a fine peak, the Ak Dagh (White Mountain), faced the camp. In late autumn it began to show a white cap above its pine forests, a warning that winter was near and that one should make preparations. Another similar warning was given by the storks which had many nests on the roofs and chimneys in the town. They had a nest on one of the camp buildings and I often watched these amusing birds and listened to their chatter. They held a conference with the 'town' storks one day, evidently fixing the date of their autumnal migration to warmer climes and then, one morning, we found that nearly all had gone. Correspondingly, in the spring, they all suddenly reappeared in their old nests, renovating them after a winter of snow damage. They announced the joyful arrival of spring by a comical display of amorous antics and house-top dances, accompanied by a clattering noise with their beaks.

Taking a hint from the departing storks, we installed iron stoves in our rooms and laid in quantities of wood brought in donkey panniers from the oak woods above the barracks. Regulating the use of these stoves needed a fine touch as they either smoked abominably or literally became red hot. In either case the small room became uninhabitable in a short time. We also laid in a stock of beans and other goods as prices began steadily to rise as a consequence of the continuation of the war and in anticipation of the approaching winter.

However the event which changed everything for the better for us was at Christmas 1917 when our numbers suddenly rose from eighteen to nearly 100 by the arrival, from another camp, of officers made prisoner at Kut who had been forced to make a difficult journey of five weeks duration in severe weather conditions. The reason for their transfer to our camp was as follows. Two or three brilliant escapes had been carried out from their camp, Kastamuni, notably one by E.H. Keeling, later an MP, who had got out and then made the hazardous journey across the Black Sea and across Russia, in the middle of its Revolution! His experiences were described in *Adventures in Turkey & Russia* (Murray 1924). This and other escapes had only succeeded because of a mixture of most careful planning, extreme fitness and an element of good luck. Most other such enterprises, some well planned and others started on the spur of the moment or even after an evening's festivities, failed at an early stage. Each of the successful, or unsuccessful, attempts resulted in the infliction of a regime of greater hardship and restrictions, including the cancellation of valuable privileges, being imposed on those recaptured and on the passive majority. Many of the officers were physically incapable of escape, which was not surprising considering the great distances and numerous obstacles which had to be overcome, not to mention the age of the senior officers.

The escapes led to a serious controversy in the camps, some officers advocating making escapes at every possible (or impossible) opportunity, sometimes just as a means of gaining relief from the boredom of captivity. Others, recognizing that their chances of escape were nil, were prepared to await the end of the war, hoping to avoid the damage to health which would result from the severity and hardship caused by the punitive regime, which was the outcome of these escapes.

The solution arrived at was that Kedos was nominated by the Turks as the camp for those willing to give an undertaking not to attempt to escape (with a reasonable option for withdrawing this form of parole later on). At Kedos a considerable degree of local freedom was to be allowed, subject to a daily evening roll call, and due notice given of any longer excursion from the vicinity of the town, when a posta would accompany the party for its guidance and protection. As medical help from Turkish sources was still inadequate, I decided to remain on, without prejudice to the representations I had made for repatriation. Two or three of our original eighteen refused to give parole and left, each with our sincere good wishes, understanding and sympathy for their motives.

We soon began to appreciate how much our lot was improved under parole conditions. The new arrivals brought with them a good library and a number of individuals turned out to be highly proficient in a variety of arts and accomplishments which proved to be of great value to the community. Two officers made violins, cellos and banjos and also taught some of us how to play. It is on record that they made sixteen banjos. Other instruments were bought and an officer who composed and orchestrated music formed an orchestra. Even though the standard of music was amateur, it was the effort which counted and what a boon it was to hear live music after being starved of it for so long. Admittedly it was a wise precaution to arrange to be out of camp when rehearsals were taking place! Then there were two accomplished artists ready to help beginners to paint and a cartoonist who showed devastating virtuosity. Another would mend your watch, if he didn't pinch the wheel out of yours to mend someone else's! Metal workers, a cobbler and a barber provided valuable practical help. Another prisoner set himself up as compiler of all news items and gave a weekly talk, illustrated by maps. This had to be done with secrecy and discretion. Godfrey Elton later Lord Elton, was one of us, as was C.L. Woolley (later Sir Leonard), the famous archaeologist, who could be just as eccentric and amusing as he was brilliant when designing theatrical costumes and settings for our Dramatic Society.

Johnny Alcock (later Sir John) deserves special mention. He had been captured when his Handley Page bomber, flying from Mudros, came down in Turkish territory. He was a dedicated airman, a true professional, who kept himself to himself and had little interest in anything but flying and longed to return to it.

> The cage is narrow and the bars are strong
> in which my restless spirit beats its wings
> and round me stretch unfathomable skies.

171

He told me in Kedos that he would be the first man to fly the Atlantic and indeed he did so in the summer of 1919, ending up in a Connemara bog, and that was eight years before Lindbergh did his solo flight. Alcock had a navigator, Whitten Brown, who was killed not long after in a trivial flight in France.

John Alcock spoke with a strong Midland accent and was at times liable to drop his aitches, which led to the following amusing incident. He and one of the orderlies were responsible one day for preparing the midday meal and laid on a rather special dish. There was plenty of it and there was some left over. The orderly asked Alcock what he should do with the remainder, to which Johnny replied 'eat it up for supper', which was just what the orderly did!

Besides making banjos the genial and versatile craftsman could act, sing and write a review. I remember one called *Kill that Bug* which was topical and, of course, bawdy, as was another version entitled *The Bride*; risqué bedroom stuff. For the latter, he compounded a lethal concoction out of raki and Greek cognac which almost destroyed some of the actors before the final curtain. He and I also made a very realistic artificial leg for our one-eyed and one-legged purveyor of liquor, an alleged victim of the Balkan Wars, but actually, I suspect the victim of some discreditable happening. The leg we made, though undoubtedly a masterpiece was very heavy and Yusep only wore it on special occasions, just as a centenarian does with his presentation set of false teeth. I believe we would have made him a false eye if we had been there longer.

The evenings when the Dramatic Society went into action were always the occasion for pretty wild celebrations but it was no bad thing for us to let our hair down and become talkative and uninhibited for a few hours, despite the inevitable hangover from the highly toxic drinks next day!

The most memorable of our stage productions undoubtedly was *Twelfth Night*, for which a most effective use was made of a wide space between the buildings, with a full moon lighting up the hillside behind and the background of a small orchard disclosing a vague statue or two. Woolley was dress designer and producer and Elton directed, as well as making a fine

Orsino. An additional encouragement was provided by a party of Turkish ladies discretely watching from a box at one side. This was a really memorable sight for all, as everyone had some hand in preparing it. Naturally, the comical antics of the two knights were strongly emphasized, rather than the romantic aspects of the play. I blush to say that I took the part of Olivia! The play inspired the following poem, written on 21 June 1918:

TWELFTH NIGHT AT KEDOS

Purple and green and white,
Deep shadows under the trees
Danced in the brazier's light
To low tuned melodies,
And the summer moon above
Shone on the hovering love.

There on the woodland stage
I saw the mummers throng,
Ghosts of a passionate age-
Heard Feste's haunting song
And dainty Viola plead,
Was this not love indeed?

We passed long hours away
With laughter and drink and song;
But the subtler spell the play
Had woven still was strong
When I wandered dreaming down
To my house in the darkened town.

What was abroad that night
As I trod the shadowy street?
The sound as if leaves fell light
Beside me – was it your feet?
Was it some drowsy bird
That sang, or your voice I heard?

'Fancies and dreams', I said,
Yet could not quite resign
Half-hopes: and then you laid
Your flower-like lips to mine
And I held you fast, and knew
It was no dream, but you.

Many other plays, revues, sketches and concerts were put on, before and after *Twelfth Night,* but they all failed to capture the original charm and illusion of that strange summer night which none of us who were there can ever forget. Feste's songs sung by C.T. Warner to music by Parsons came softly echoing from the walls of the adjoining buildings on the night air to complete the enchantment.

But before all this we had to live through a dark and bitter winter when our chains seemed to weigh heavily upon us. Even the parcels from our people at home and from the Red Cross seemed to pile up longer than ever away at Ouchak. The news from Flanders of the great March offensive launched by the Germans added to my gloom as I had a brother with Gough's Army in France [ed. this was Maurice Spackman].

When spring did arrive, quite suddenly, our Field Club, which catered for a wide range of interests, did much to mitigate such moods and dispel depression by encouraging activity outside the camp and barracks. We took full advantage of the freedom granted to us in response to our giving our parole. Some of us went climbing or exploring in the wild and hilly country around us. Others preferred to walk or sketch below the town beside the river, said to have been the Meander of the classics, where on a hot afternoon one might find a cool pool for a swim. Butterflies and flowers were collected and studied and the great variety of bird life in the area provided another interest.

I was one of the keen walkers and climbers, making friends with the muktars (official headmen) of the mountain villages, and going out on Sundays with the villagers, hunting wild boar in the high forests. For us, the beaters, it meant much toiling up, down and across the winding paths and slopes, past the charcoal burners' clearings and through the snow drifts. We found tracks of wild pig often enough but rarely bagged one.

These hunting parties were made up of elderly men and young boys, with usually one or two soldiers on sick leave after suffering wounds or sickness. When we sat down at noon to eat our meal we might well be joined in the wilder country areas by a man who might be a deserter, or a fugitive from justice who had been accepted by the villagers. With their diverse range of clothes and arms the hunters made an interesting study and I wished I had a camera to record the scene (but would not have dared to use it, even if I had one).

On one memorable occasion when I was out with the men from our favourite village of Akchallan, high under the Ak Dagh, two pigs were shot. Pork is a forbidden meat for Moslems, so I bought the carcasses for a small sum, had them cut up, and transported them to the barracks in donkey baskets, where they made a welcome addition to the menu. I reserved a good ham for myself for use at a private party.

Johnny Alcock had a nasty experience when out on one of our cross-country walks. We were traversing a hillside and typically he was taking a slightly different line from the other three of us when he was set upon by several ferocious sheep dogs. These dogs, resembling Alsatians, have rough, tough coats and are used to protect sheep from wolves, but will always attack strangers. Some of us knew how to deal with them by keeping together and arming ourselves with stout sticks. Another way was to throw sticks or bowl large stones at them when they would turn their rage against the missile instead of upon the intruder!

Alcock, unfortunately, did not know about this dodge. The dogs charged him and got him down and, if we had not been near enough to rush to his rescue and beat off the brutes, he might have been killed. We were relieved to find he had got off with a few minor bites but had received a lot of damage to his clothes.

Johnny's Canadian observer, Aird, was one of the camp's wags. On first arriving at the camp at Kedos after the usual long journey, he had begun to grow a beard by which he was then easily recognized from afar.

Towards the end of March 1918 all kinds of rumours, true and false, were circulated as the fighting on various fronts flared up, especially that involving the German partial breakthrough against Gough's Fifth Army. News that reached us was most confusing; disasters in France in one sector and triumphs in other spheres of war. We didn't know what to believe, though occasionally we received a single sheet of paper called *Hillal* printed in French in Constantinople which gave us heavily biased and unreliable news.

On 31 March a report got about – no one took the trouble to trace its source – that a newly captured airman was expected to arrive in the camp any day, so no one was surprised when a dirty and dishevelled officer, in a ragged infantry uniform, turned up in our Mess next day. A special meal was prepared for him, a serviceable collection of clothes provided and a loan of £5 arranged. Quite a crowd naturally collected around him when he gave what would now be known as a press conference and we listened with rapt attention to the many items of 'news' he recounted. Much of it was past history and common knowledge but as he went on his tales began to be more unexpected and surprising, towns captured and advances made which made us at first elated, in our innocence, and then led us to be more questioning. Finally someone asked him how long he had been on his journey since capture. 'Let's see,' he enquired, 'this is the 31 March isn't it?', to which we, all born April Fools, replied 'No, it's 1 April', and then the penny dropped. It was, of course, Aird minus his beard and specially dressed up.

The main reason for the success of this hoax was due to the fact that, with the large influx of officers at Christmas from other camps, much fresh accommodation had to be found, including a great main khan in the town centre and several hired houses for smaller groups. Aird had then moved from the barracks to one of the smaller houses where he was out of sight.

Following this prank, Gus Rae increased the activity of his news centre and various ingenious codes were invented to get news in and out of the camp.

Example. In a letter home: 'Any news about Uncle Sam and what he expects to do? Douglas's exam must be soon, does he hope to pass? I hear that Namso is sure he made a mistake when he was sold that pup by William and he should have taken George's instead'. The identities of Uncle Sam and Douglas (Haig), William (the Kaiser), and King George are obvious enough. Namso spelt backwards is Osman, the Turks being Osmanlis. I don't think much was achieved by such elementary codes but it afforded fun devising them.

One of our officers at Kedos, named Cheshire, was a most useful person because he had taught himself the art of mending shoes. Apart from working at his last, he was never known to take any exercise whatever. One day the onbashi (corporal), whose duty it was to conduct shopping parties round the town, came along as usual, shouting 'Charshiya, charshiya'! Thinking he was being summoned to the Commandant's office, Cheshire obediently got up off his last, leaving a re-soling job unfinished, and followed the corporal, who took him on a long and complicated tour of all the shops in the town which we patronized, becoming more puzzled and bewildered at each one. At each shop, Cheshire said 'yok' (no), which was the only word of Turkish he knew, so the corporal, with a resigned and questioning 'yok', led the perspiring Cheshire on to yet another shop. Finally he brought him back exhausted and empty handed to the barracks and to his deserted last, when someone explained to him that 'Charshiya' simply meant 'to the town'. Poor Cheshire was known as 'Charshiya' thereafter.

What might be called the great final drama of our sojourn at Kedos centred around and finally cut short our production, at the end of September 1918, of a musical show called *Theodore and Company*. We already had acquired the score of the *Maid of the Mountains* and had recently received, courtesy of the Dutch Ambassador in Constantinople, the score of the *Gipsy Princess*, a famous new hit from Vienna. To these scores were added bits and pieces from other stage shows from Daly's Theatre and the Gaiety, remembered by officers and then hummed to Parsons who incorporated them into a cheerful song and dance show, tied in to a simple plot requiring no mental effort from the audience to follow.

There can hardly have been anyone in the camp who was not drawn in to the work of preparing for this production. Old Colonel Taylor became heavily involved because of his knowledge of melodies, words and stage craft. Taylor was the only officer who knew anything about stage routines for female chorus dances and it was comic to see how, in his sudden enthusiasm, he forgot his disabilities while demonstrating to us some quite athletic steps and high kicks. This might have been embarrassing to me as in August I had been asked to select some officers for possible repatriation on an exchange basis as unfit for further military duty and the Turkish doctor and I had included Taylor on the list on the strength of a damaged right knee. Also he looked old for his age and we had been unable to find many others among the officers and orderlies whose poor health justified inclusion.

It was uncanny how, using basic materials such as canvas coverings from our parcels, old mosquito nets, the gauze from surgical dressings, bazaar dyes, etc. we managed to make costumes, skirts, frills, hats and accessories for the large cast. The West End could not have done better! The hats were contrived from a rigid basis of glue and canvas shaped over a clay mould and the wigs were made out of goats' hair. The Maison Woolley became an intriguing sight to visit, with muscular 'actresses' being fitted into ballet skirts and others into wigs, furs and costumes amidst the blare of musical instruments being tuned, practised or beaten.

In the middle of this feverish activity we were struck by the great epidemic of influenza which was soon to spread so tragically westward with appalling results. Fortunately it had not attained the virulence it later developed but it threw our timetable out of gear, causing interruptions and delays in all departments. I had a busy time, rushing to our people all over town for days on end with aspirin and other simple palliatives. To complicate the situation, the opening day for the production had to be advanced when orders were received for Colonel Taylor and the other invalids to proceed to Constantinople for repatriation!

178

By now the fame of our Dramatic Society was known far and wide so that, long before the curtain was due to rise, the entire population of Kedos came pouring into the grounds. Near one corner of the outdoor stage a special bower had been discretely arranged, as was customary, for the Turkish ladies of Edhem Bey's party, who could be heard gaily chattering and occasionally glimpsed, among the flowers and plants we had provided to shield them from prying eyes. The date was 27 September 1918, the weather fine and dry, with an appreciable breeze.

Our play was in three acts and, with encores; the show was estimated to run for four hours. None of our productions had to be constrained by any consideration of time! The male and 'female' choruses performed prodigies of coordinated dancing, the orchestra under Parsons excelled itself and the principals performed with spontaneous élan. The whole show promised to be a tour de force, and was acclaimed by an appreciative and enthusiastic audience.

The second act ended, after several encores, with a chorus written for the show which turned out to be curiously appropriate:

> We'll never come back no more, boys,
> Never come back no more!
> Shut up the old shop window, put a notice over the door,
> We're packing our kits for the jolly old Ritz,
> And we'll never come back no more!

The stage company then retired for well earned refreshments but while the stage effects for the triumphant third act were being assembled and installed, news reached the camp that a serious fire had started in the centre of Kedos. The first hint we received of this was that the large Turkish element of our audience, who were sitting or standing mainly in the background, started to melt silently away.

It became evident later that an old Turkish woman in a house in the crowded quarter of the town next to the khan (which housed many of the British officers and orderlies) had been boiling up some grape juice on a charcoal brazier when she

179

accidentally upset it and started a conflagration which might, I suppose, have been easily extinguished had not all the able-bodied men been up at the concert at the time.

It had been an exceptional dry summer and consequently most of the small streams and fountains in the town had run dry or been reduced to a trickle. The houses were constructed of wood and mud-brick and huddled together along narrow alleyways. This recipe for disaster was not helped by the fact that the town fire engine was an antiquated and ineffective hand-pump contraption mounted on a rickety trolley, equipped with a short length of leaky hose! A light but gusty wing had sprung up to fan the flames. Added to all this, it took some time for the alarm to be raised in our camp which was a good half a mile away. The result was a foregone conclusion. The fire took hold and the huge khan and all the houses around it were soon blazing furiously. The British personnel billeted there lost every-thing and our precious library went up in flames.

The consequence was that the third act with its glittering triumphant conclusion, so carefully rehearsed, was never performed. The audience and the cast mingled in one tumul-tuous rabble rushing to the town, the actors in their costumes and the 'chorus girls' in their ballet skirts jostling with each other in their haste to try to see what could be saved both for the British personnel and for the Turks. For, in an emergency such as this, the efforts of the Turkish population to save their property was pitiable and they, recognizing the energy and organized efficiency of the British Army, soon called upon us to save their homes and their goods from the flames, which had now started to spread in all directions. The town became a raging furnace. No one could approach the khan or the other houses in which our men lived. Attempts to control the flames with water were clearly doomed to failure and were quickly abandoned in favour of trying to save what could be dragged out of the houses not yet engulfed, such items being transported well away from the danger area regardless of ownership.

An immediate attempt to limit the spread of the fire by creating fire-breaks by pulling down some ramshackle dwellings, was frustrated by their hysterical owners (the houses

180

soon burned down anyway), but late in the night, by which time our efforts had secured the backing if not the active cooperation of the local civil authorities, a few houses towards the outskirts were saved by these means. These houses, with some others more remotely situated, were all that remained intact at dawn among the smoking ruins of the town, all the rest having become smouldering and malodorous rubbish. One satisfactory feature was that there had been no loss of life, so far as anyone was aware.

The theatrical show followed by the spectacular fire made this a day never to be forgotten! What lives in the memory were the thrill and triumph of the stage show, so eagerly worked for by all for weeks beforehand, and the Dante-esque spectacle of the great midnight fire, with actors in their fancy stage costumes and the ballet girls in the brief frills, half-choked with smoke and dust, grimly struggling until long after dawn to rescue what they could from the burning town, amid the alternate prayers and curses of the completely ineffectual local population.

Dawn saw groups of exhausted officers and orderlies amid the smoking ruins still toiling to rescue and then sort out their own and the townspeople's few remaining possessions. One young officer, who had lost all his everyday clothing in the fire, wearily spent all the next day in his dishevelled ballet dress, having spent the night pulling down houses in the part of the town directly in the path of the flames. In the official Turkish account of the Kedos fire it was stated that whatever items were saved in the entire town was solely due to the efforts of the British prisoners of war.

Chapter Nineteen

Never Come Back No More

So that, for us, was the end of our sojourn at Kedos. A dull little town deep in the mountains of Asia Minor, it was rebuilt the following year on more substantial lines. However that was not the end of its troubles for it lay at the centre of the fighting in the Greco-Turkish war in 1921-22 when Mustapha Kemal, the Grey Wolf, rebuilt the Turkish Army and Nation and drove out the Greeks with fire and bayonet. Perhaps Kedos (by now called Gediz) may even have been burnt down yet again, as happened to much of Smyrna in that bloody campaign.

Leonard Woolley had told us that the town was of great antiquity but I believe that much of its history was crowded into those few years from 1917 to 1922. Even today schoolteachers are probably recounting to their students tales of those momentous days and that disastrous night, and of how a few British prisoners of war tried to save the burning town.

The immediate result of the fire, as far as we were concerned, was that accommodation had to be found both for the inhabitants and for those British who had lived in the hired houses and the khan, all of which had gone. The Turkish population packed up what was left of their possessions and carried them off to nearby villages or to more distant towns by pony transport or on their heads and backs, a melancholy exodus, repeated daily. The prisoners of war crowded into the barrack camp. Provisions became scarce, prices rose sharply and the situation became critical. Yet it took the authorities in Constantinople over a fortnight to order a move to a new town, which was a considerable distance away. Meanwhile, in view of the near approach of winter, a preliminary move to Ouchak was authorized, where the British could be accommodated in railway buildings and sheds. During this move the column encountered some brigands and one officer was slightly wounded. No material loss was sustained. Within a few days of this move the course of the war took a dramatic turn. Bulgaria collapsed and made peace with the Allies. Turkey found itself isolated from Germany and sued for peace which resulted in the end of hostilities. Orders were then given for all prisoners of war in the interior of Anatolia to be sent to Smyrna, whence they would be repatriated by sea to Egypt and thence homewards.

Before this general move from Kedos was authorized, a surprising event had befallen me. The old order for my repatriation from Baghdad, and the protest I had made from Kedos, had at last worked their way through the system and an order was issued for me to be sent to Smyrna to join a few others, mainly invalids, who were awaiting exchange. Since the flu epidemic was over, the end of the war was evidently close at hand and a competent Turkish doctor had replaced the old inefficient one, I felt no need to stay and departed with 'a song in my heart'.

I shamelessly raised some cash by selling most of my possessions (for which I found a good market) and with the proceeds gave a farewell party. By bartering a good deal of cognac and raki, I engaged some of our orchestra for entertainment and gave a few of my friends supper, followed by dancing among ourselves on the outside stage. It was a lovely night but, as the night wore on, one by one members of the band succumbed, and my last recollection of the occasion was of the violinist, the last survivor, propped up against a post at the corner of the stage scraping away at his instrument without regard for tune or rhythm but with a beatific smile on his face. Next day I left for Ouchak with such a cruel hangover that I remember little about that journey. Those spirits were lethal!

So to Smyrna I went, under guard but in comparative comfort. There I was given quarters in the American Mission College at Paradiso on the outskirts of the town, where a number of old crocks and invalids were being assembled for exchange from various camps and hospitals. Among those were two old Kut acquaintances of mine, Hill and Jones, the famous authors of the book *The Road to Endor* which tells of how they feigned the ability to get in touch with the spirit world and to receive messages through a 'ouija' board and the fantastic story of the 'insanity' which overcame them, when they acted so successfully that they convinced both the Turks and their British comrades that they were hopelessly and dangerously insane. After some ghastly experiences in Turkish lunatic asylums they had been sent down to Smyrna for repatriation. I saw Hill arrive at Paradiso and admit that I would have signed him up for an asylum! Dirty and unkempt, he was reading or thumbing over, the tattered remains of a Bible. It was said that he spent his whole day doing this. After being helped out of the araba in which he had arrived, he subsided at once onto the ground by a wall and went on with his reading, taking no apparent interest in anything, nor of any old friends who tried to talk to him, even though the whole camp was agog with the joyful news that the war with Turkey was over. He did not relax his 'mad' behaviour until he was carried onto a British transport in the Gulf of Smyrna when he made an immediate and apparently complete recovery! Two or three years later, he flew his own aeroplane in a solo flight from Australia to England!

There was a colony of wealthy Levantine merchants, chiefly British and French, the Whittals, Girauds and Lafontaines, much inter-related, living a quiet and unmolested life in the pretty villages of Boudja and Bournabat above Smyrna, who opened their doors to us with great kindness and hospitality. With the almost complete relaxation of the restrictions of captivity which had occurred, we soon made a lot of friends and were invited by these kind people to take part in entertainments and parties. The Vali of Smyrna at that time was one Rahmy Bey, a patriotic Turk but a very intelligent friend of the British as well. I met him several times both at his own home and at the house of Charles Giraud with whom I was staying at Bournabat. Rahmy was a collector of oriental carpets, furniture and curios with which his house was grossly overburdened. He gave me a very ornate Persian Dagger inscribed on its curved blade with the somewhat unexpected words to find on such a weapon 'Allah is Merciful'.

We were not favourably impressed by the behaviour of the large Greek population on the whole. They were noisy, bombastic and boastful and behaved badly to the unfortunate Turkish officials who had found themselves on the losing side and in the unpleasant position of lacking all real authority on the civil side yet having to keep order with a few disheartened troops and gendarmes. On one occasion we were able to rescue a senior Turkish officer who was being beaten up by a riotous Greek mob. To our surprise he turned out to be Nureddin Pasha, our old opponent in the early days of fighting on the Tigris.

An ever recurring theme in my conversations with Rahmy and the Levantine merchants was the fear that the Greek leader Venezelos might persuade the Allies to hand over Smyrna and a substantial area of the hinterland to the Greeks after the war. It was believed that the councils in London and Paris were being swayed by the non-conformist supporters of Lloyd George, whilst those in Washington were listening to the urgings of President Wilson's Quaker friends. Their viewpoint was that the Greeks were allies of ours, albeit pretty unreliable at times, and moreover were Christians, whereas the Turks had been enemies and were infidels; therefore the Greeks should be given everything for which they asked.

I already was aware that, for historical reasons, the Turks would never allow the annexation of Smyrna and its villages by Greece and that, until the Greeks living there were forcibly thrown out, there would be unending disorder. My friends urged me to convey these views to the British Foreign Office as strongly as possible as soon as I got to London. This indeed I did. I was listened to politely and then bowed out without comment. The sequel is a matter of history. Turkey was dismembered at the end of the war, except for her homelands in Anatolia, by the Treaty of Sevres. The occupation of Smyrna and much of Anatolia behind it was more than the proud Turks could stand. Kemal Ataturk denounced the terms of the treaty, reunited his faithful Turks, drilled and organized them for two years and finally confronted the Greeks at Afion on the 25

185

August 1922. After a desperate battle lasting five days and after throwing in his ultimate reserves, he totally defeated the Greek Army, which fled in disorder towards Smyrna and the sea, laying waste the countryside in their retreat and burning the towns of Afion, Ouchak, Alashehir and Manissa. Kemal and his victorious army carried out a hot pursuit of the Greeks, reaching Smyrna on 9 September, chasing the last remnants literally into the sea. Large parts of Smyrna were burnt out in a great fire which consumed a million pounds' worth of carpets in the warehouses of the Oriental Carpet Company. Hundreds of civilians perished, including some members of the Levantine colony I knew, and many more lost all that they possessed.

After this the Allies had no choice but to scrap the Treaty of Sevres and sign a new one which recognized the Government at Ankara as the official Government of Turkey and restored Smyrna and Thrace to Turkey again.

Returning our story to October 1918, my memories of Smyrna are of much noise and some turmoil in the town, with bombastic processions and demonstrations by Greeks parading huge pictures of Venezelos through the streets, of parties and dancing in the Kraemer Palace Hotel on the waterfront, and of the peace and friendliness I met at Bournabat. Also of a moonlight party in a boat off Cordelio (the place where Richard Coeur de Lion landed) and of a fat, ugly little man who sang to us romantic Greek songs in a fine tenor voice to the accompaniment of his own mandolin and the ripple of the waves, his face transfigured as he sang to the moon with his whole heart. We did not understand the words, probably they were sadly banal, but this was probably one of the supreme hours of his uneventful life. Romance was in the air just then and at one merchant's house over at Cordelio my charming hostess alarmed me by showing so much 'friendliness' that I, like a coward, accepted an invitation to stay elsewhere!

We went into town every day to find out if there was any news of the promised exchange ship, for we were getting more and more impatient to end our captivity, mitigated as it now was. There was really not much delay. The steamer from Alexandria had been tasked to carry out the exchange of invalids many weeks before the Armistice with Turkey had been signed. The Turkish Armistice took effect on 1 November 1918, preceding the Armistice in France by ten days.

On 5 November a British Monitor steamed into the harbour and took over the port, together with the rusty collection of shipping which was tied up to its quays. With her White Ensign flying, she received an enthusiastic welcome from us and from the whole town, including some Turkish naval officers; by tradition closely associated with the Royal Navy and now only too ready to forget the immediate past. All available tugs and launches were assembled and, on 11 November, with great excitement, we embarked in them and sailed away down the Gulf, threading a devious path through alleged minefields until, on rounding a headland, we came upon a lovely white ship at anchor in the calm waters.

But there had been a mistake somewhere! The SS *Assaye* was a hospital ship and was not intended to take more than a certain number of patients. A few extra could be taken but not all that had been brought out and so I was selected to return to shore accompanied by about forty Indians who had remained in the launches. I went aboard to protest, in vain, but did succeed in getting a few baskets of food for the Indians. While I was signing for these, deep in the bowels of the ship, the gangway was hauled up and the ship weighed. The last load of provisions was hastily dumped over the side and I climbed down one of the precarious pilot's ladders into a little cockle-shell boat and watched the hardhearted Captain sail his steamer away.

My disconsolate little party reached Smyrna again at about midnight, quite unexpected and unprepared for, and spent what was left of the night, rather resentfully on the part of some of the Indians, in some sheds beside the quay. We were soon living in comfort again and were joined by many other prisoners from more distant camps. We had not long to wait and, waving a grateful farewell once more to our newly made friends on the quayside, were soon setting sail in a fresh expedition to Fokia where HMT *Empire* was waiting for us. Rumour has it that several tearful women were sad to see us go, a reminder of the tradition established by Richard Coeur de Lion long ago when romances between the followers of Mars and Venus were quite acceptable to the inhabitants of that classic land.

What rejoicing there was to see the Blue Ensign fluttering from the stern of the transport. More than thirty months had passed since we saw Major General Townshend haul down the Union Jack at Kut in token of surrender. In that time our numbers had declined from 12,000 to about one third of that total, the rest having perished.

So our little boats fussily manoeuvred towards the gangway that represented escape from captivity and the promise of a new life, offering opportunity and adventure (as indeed proved to be the case). We turned for a last look at those distant shores, gleaming in the afternoon sunlight, and someone started to sing the old song written in Kedos camp, taken up happily by the rest of us – 'We'll never come back no more, boys, never come back no more!'

I left Fokia (Gulf of Smyrna) on HMT *Empire* on 18 November 1918, arriving at Alexandria on 21 November. I met my brother Charles (RAMC) in Alexandria on 3 December, leaving Alexandria on the *Caledonia* on 5 December, disembarking Marseilles on 10 December, travelling overland to Calais, Dover and London.

Postscript

November 1970 – Fifty Years On

That promise was not kept by me, at least. In spite of the song I did go back fifty years later, aged 78, in March 1967. In response to an inexplicable impulse, I made the journey from Istanbul by train to Kutahieh and then continued in a broken down Vauxhall taxi driven by a bewhiskered taxi man across the mountains in a blizzard from Kutahieh to Kedos. My only means of communication with the inhabitants during the three day trip from Istanbul was in my rusty and ill-remembered Turkish, but it sufficed to identify me and to tell my simple story, which was embellished and loudly proclaimed to all prepared to listen by my taxi man, who appointed himself my publicity agent!

Kedos did not seem much changed as we drove down the main street and stopped at a coffee house, except for a group of mini-buses bearing the names of local villages, one from Akchallan. Kedos had now become Gediz and boasted a motel, a thermal spring and a cinema! There were a lot of people in the coffee house, it being market day, mainly sitting around the central iron stove on benches, and when my taxi man importantly announced my arrival and credentials they crowded around me showing great interest in this throw-back from the past. Two or three old men gained reflected glory by remembering and recounting stories of the Great Fire of September 1918.

I then visited the site of the old barracks. The football field was now occupied by two-storey school buildings, built in a plain modern style, whilst staff quarters had replaced the barracks. The old guard room looked unchanged, except for an electricity pylon in front of it.

The schoolboys came pouring out, dressed in long trousers and jackets much like schoolboys anywhere and surrounded me, trying out phrases in English or French in response to my halting Turkish, which caused them much amusement. I gave them a small Union Jack which delighted them. All the time my 'publicity man' was proclaiming my fame as a man resurrected from the historical past and it was only with difficulty that I was able to get away for my return by taxi, in better weather, to Kutahieh in time to catch the evening train back to Istanbul.

It is a sad fact that only three years later the town and surrounding villages were totally destroyed, with much loss of life, in the disastrous earthquake centred just there in March 1970.

Appendix 1

Letter home from Dr Charles Spackman, RMO, 1 Manchester Regiment, part of the Relief Force, 3rd Division, Tigris Army Corps. 10 March 1916:

My dearest Mother,

We have just come out of a terrific attack on the Dujailah Redoubt of the Es Sinn position held by the Turk. Alas, today we are back at the Wadi camp. After marching all night of the 7 March, we were kept hanging about two miles in front of the 'show' with artillery bombardments going on. We were Brigade in reserve. Attacks during the day having been unsuccessful, the Brigade was brought up (8 March). At 1630 hrs General Keary, 3 Indian Div (Lahore) spoke to the officers impressively and it seemed to me sadly. As you will see if the sketch I sent is allowed through, the regiment attacked at about 1715 hrs against the setting sun and I got a fine view from behind a small mound which with the aid of a spade we made just sufficient head cover well within rifle fire.

It was a glorious sight to see the battalion opening out and advancing with live fire kicking up the dust and then the salvos of Turkish shrapnel bursting in line all across the field, with our own artillery fire at the Redoubt itself. I could see our men reaching the Redoubt and dropping in on the skyline and thought the attack was to be successful, no other battalion having got in at all. Alas, after some time we saw them retiring, streams of wounded getting back as best they could still under heavy fire. Some of my stretcher bearers and I went up about 1815 hrs well before the light had failed, so as to see better for getting the men back and it was ticklish work as there were plenty of bullets about. However we were lucky in only getting one man hit in the leg. I found Gowen-Smith, who had been my 'bedding pal' in small tents here and in France, paralysed in both legs, poor chap. He thought he was dying – another was shot in three places and we got him in too. It was risky work, as we were fired on often and could hear the Turks (and possibly Arabs) within a couple of hundred yards as all our troops had retired and everyone in the Field Ambulance had 'wind up' of a Turk attack, we had to go cautiously and were lucky in having a slight moon. By 2200 hrs I was done in* and I slept like a log in the sand while other parties carried on the good work. Between 200 and 300 of our men (wounded) have got back here so I don't think many were left (censored).

I myself heard and saw the flash of a rifle fired into the ground 150 yards off – I can't swear that the former information is correct but I think we would have been foolish to go further.

At 1800 hrs a retirement began, the wounded convoy measuring over a mile in length, we lost about 500 all told (censored) officers, only four of which were evacuated wounded so you can see it has been a terrible blow.

A march all day of about twelve miles, carried out in the blazing sun was very trying after forty-eight hours with little sleep or water and naturally a good many of the wounded (censored). Well, dearest mother, I have got through all right when so many gallant boys have gone under – had we attacked in the early morn I feel sure we should have taken and held the position. Well I hope to send better news next time – my hopes of seeing brother Will in a few days were badly shaken.

Much love your affectionate son, Charles.
P.S. Got yours giving details of Will's bad time the other day.

*Editors note: Charles Spackman was, himself, wounded during the attack but insisted on going back to rescue the wounded. He was put in for an immediate DSO by Lieutenant Colonel Hardcastle, CO 1st Manchester Regiment, but it was turned down.

Appendix 2

Historical Summary, Mesopotamian Campaign

1914

16 October. The 6th (Poona) Division, Indian Army, comprising 16, 17 and 18 Brigades embarked from Bombay, including 2 Dorsets, 1 Oxford and Buckingham LI and 2 Norfolks. The 48th Pioneers strength was 15 officers and 700 rank and file.

23 October. The Force disembarked at Bahrain. The aim was to secure the oil port of Basra and secure communications in the Shatt al Arab.

11 November. First action. Capture of the Shatt al Arab peninsula.

23 November. Capture of Basra. Filthy town of 60,000 inhabitants, infested with flies. Divisional Commander, Major General Sir A Barrett. Command was divided between the Government of India and the War Office. The campaign was based on river transport up the Euphrates to the west and the Tigris to the east. The weather was scorching by day, chilly by night, and the plains flooded in spring. Qurna was stormed, over 1,000 Turks captured, 27 British killed, 292 wounded. No further action took place in the winter but a second Division was sent from India, 12 Division, Commander Major General Gorringe.

1915

9 April. Lieutenant General Sir John Nixon succeeded to overall command.

15 April. Battle of Shaiba. Decisive battle, encouraged the Command to advance with a force of two Divisions and a Cavalry Brigade.

22 April. Major General Charles Vere Ferrer Townshend, CB, DSO, aged 54, took over as Commander of 6th Division. Brigadier General Roberts commanded the Cavalry Brigade.

4 June. Amara was captured by 6th (Indian) Division. Large town. Easy victory led to overconfidence. Summer heat of 120-130 deg F. Insects appalling.

27 June. 12 Div assaulted and captured Nasiriyeh. Turks withdrew towards Kut al Amara. British Force now 200 miles from sea, was suffering from sickness, depression and lack of medical supplies.

15 September. Captured Abu Rammaneh (1,700 prisoners, 3 guns). The Cavalry Brigade took Aziziyeh, 50 miles further on. Turks held Es Sinn position, below Kut.

26 September. Force assaulted and captured Kut, 280 miles from the sea. Defeated the Turks commanded by General Nur-ud-din. Sir John Nixon could not resist going for Baghdad and prepared to advance on Ctesiphon.

21 November. Townshend attacked Ctesiphon, only 16 miles from Baghdad but 400 miles from the sea, with 8,500 troops, outnumbered 3:1 by the Turks, whose reinforcements were only 22 miles away. Half of Townsend's force was killed or wounded; the battle was indecisive, there were inadequate medical facilities (by boat to Basra), boiling days and cold nights.

25 November. The retreat to Kut began through Lajj and Aziziyeh. The Turks under Field Marshal von der Goltz (German) had 30,000 reinforcements on the way. The British had three more Divisions in the theatre under Sir Fenton Aylmer, Corps Commander. Major General Maude commanded 13th Division.

5 December. The Siege of Kut began. Thirteen thousand British and Indian troops besieged by 80,000 Turks and Arabs. Townshend was advised to withdraw by the Cabinet, but too late.

10 December. The Battle of the Kut Fort. The Turks were driven out at bayonet point.

1916

January/March. Continuous battles between Goltz and Lieutenant General Fenton Aylmer, VC's, Relief Force. At the Battle of Sheik Sa'id, 4,000 Relief Force personnel were killed or wounded. Terrible medical problems – hospital ships on the Tigris were 'hell on earth'.

13 January. Battle of Wadi.

21 January. Battle of Hanna. At these two battles 6,000 men were lost and the Relief Force turned back. Only 46 guns were available. During a six-hour 'truce', Arabs stripped and murdered the wounded.

21 January. Serious floods in Kut turned both sides' lines into a sea of mud.

7/8 March. A further major relief attempt was made. (See Appendix 1). It turned the main Turkish position at Es Sinn after striking across the desert, attacking Dujailah Redoubt, two miles from Kut, but was then driven back with 3,500 casualties. It featured poor tactics, daylight open attacks, heroic actions, and many decorations. Fenton was replaced by Lieutenant General Gorringe, on promotion.

Late March. Nixon removed from Command, replaced by General Sir Percy Lake.

Between 4 Dec. 1915 and 31 Mar. 1916. In the Kut perimeter, the 48th Pioneers had two British officers wounded, one Indian officer missing, seventeen rank and file killed, twenty-two men died of wounds, eighty-three were wounded and sixteen died of disease.

25 April. A last ditch attempt by the ship *Julnar* failed to break through to Kut with supplies. By now 23,000 men had been killed or wounded in various attempts to rescue a garrison of half that size. No word of thanks from Townshend to the Relief Force was received.

27 April. A Government offer of £1M in gold to release the Kut troops was rejected by the Turks/Germans. One report quotes the figure as £2M.

29 April. Townshend surrendered Kut. Siege had lasted 147 days.

30 April. Approx 12,000 men were taken into captivity. Approx 345 or more badly wounded or sick men were exchanged for Turkish prisoners (figure unconfirmed).

Between 22 November 1914 and the Fall of Kut. 35,000 British and Indian troops were killed or wounded in Mesopotamia.

6 May. The death march began over 15 miles without water or shade and the captives were beaten by captors in appalling heat.

18 May. The first party reached Baghdad. After three days in a compound without shade or sanitation, they marched on. A train took General Townshend with his servants to Constantinople and thence to an island residence where he remained in comfort till the war end. After the war he referred to this time as 'having been an honoured guest of the Turks'!

Thereafter, of the 2,500 British troops captured at Kut, 1,750 died on the march or in POW camps. Of the 9,300 Indian troops captured at Kut 2,500 died on the march or in camps.

Summer/Autumn. The British Mesopotamian Army was re-organized and prepared for battle by General Sir Stanley Maude who improved his base at Basra and his supply lines. Only then did he embark on an extremely cautious offensive.

12 December. New offensive began up the Tigris with 50,000 men.

1917

1 February. Maude prepared to attack Kut, garrisoned by 12,000 Turks.

24 February. British and Indian troops recaptured Kut, taking 1,730 POW.

5 March. The advance reached Aziziyeh. The Turks abandoned their lines without a fight, forced out by skilful deployment.

11 March. The Cavalry Division, VII Corps, entered Baghdad, taking 9,000 POW.

Commenting on and comparing the two campaigns, Townshend's and Maude's, a renowned historian writes:

And if quality rather than quantity be the test of a feat of arms, comparison suggests that the advance and retreat of Townshend's original 6th (Indian) Division, in face of superior numbers, with inadequate equipment, primitive communications and utterly isolated in the heart of an enemy country, forged an intrinsically finer link in the chain of British military history.

Appendix 3

Order of Battle, 6th Indian Division in Kut Forces besieged at Kut under Major General Townshend, CB, DSO, on 3 December 1915

(The operational strength of units was greatly reduced by casualties and sickness)

HQ 6th Indian Division
16 Infantry Bde
2 Bn Dorset Regt.
66th Punjabis
104th Wellesley's Rifles
117th Mahrattas

17 Infantry Bde
1st Bn Ox & Bucks Lt Inf
22nd Punjabis
103th Mahratta Lt Inf
119th Rajputana Inf

18 Infantry Bde
2nd Bn Norfolk Regt
7th Rajputs
110th Mahratta Lt Inf
120th Rajputana Inf

30 Infantry Bde (12 Division)
1/2 Bn 2nd R West Kent Regt

Divisional & Army Troops

Royal Artillery
S Bty R Horse Artillery, 1 Section
10th Bde, R Field Artillery:
  63,76,82 Btys (18 pdrs)
1/5th Hants Howitzer Bty (T)
R Garrison Artillery 86 Heavy Bty
104th Heavy Bty, 1 Section
Vol Arty Bty Rangoon (15 pdr)
6th Div Ammo Column

Royal Engineers
17 & 22 Coys 3rd Sappers & Miners
Bridging Train
Sirmoor Sapper Coy
Searchlight Section

Royal Corps of Signals
34 Signal Coy, 30 Bde Signals
Wireless Signal Coy

1 Coy 1/4th Hampshire Regt
24th Punjabis   **Cavalry**
67th Punjabis   One Squadron 23 Cavalry
76th Punjabis   One Squadron 7th Lancers
2/7th Gurkha Rifles

                                 Infantry
                                 48th Pioneers
                                 Machine Gun Coy

Administrative Troops
3 x Field Ambulances   Transport Units
3 x Field Hospitals   Animal Detachments, Mule Corps
1 Section Veterinary Hospital   Mechanical Transport Corps

Royal Navy
HMS *Sumara* (River Gunboat)
4 x Horse Boats (4,7" gun in each)

Detachment R. Flying Corps

Surrender, 29 April 1916
10,061 combatants surrendered:
(277 British & 204 Indian officers,
2,592 British & 6,988 Indian other ranks).
plus 3,248 Indian non-combatants
Total 13,309

Appendix 4

The 48th Pioneers, Indian Army

The Pioneer Regiments in the Indian Army were classed as Infantry Regiments but had additional roles such as road-making and the construction of defences.

In the mid-nineteenth century in India there were three separate Presidency Armies; those of Bengal, Madras and Bombay. Then, in 1903, the battalions were brought together onto one consecutively numbered list of which the Bengal Infantry were numbers 1 to 48 and the last, the Bombay Infantry, being numbered 101 to 130. Thus the 48th Pioneers were the last raised Bengal Infantry regiment (in 1901), before the reorganization of the Indian Army in 1903.

In the Bengal order of battle the 23rd, 32nd and 34th were Sikh Pioneers but the 48th were mixed class with Jats, Hindustani Mussulmans, Lobana Sikhs etc., all in class companies.

Many British Officers in the Indian Army volunteered to serve in Pioneer Regiments because on every campaign there was always at least one such regiment included in the order of battle. The continuous deployments on the North-West and North-East Frontiers (sometimes only one battalion plus one Pioneer Battalion) more or less guaranteed that Pioneer Regiments saw more service than any others.

The 48th Pioneers, being the most recently raised, did not have such a long record of service, and their captivity in Kut also reduced their opportunities for gaining further distinction.

In late 1916 the 48th were reconstituted and a second battalion

(2nd/48th Pioneers) was formed in India in 1918. After a series of reorganizations, one of which put the 12th and 48th Pioneers within the 2nd Bombay Pioneers where the 48th became the 4th Battalion, 2nd Bombay Pioneers, finally the 4th/2nd Bombay Pioneers were disbanded in 1926, the original 48th having only existed from 1901 to 1926.

Index

205